A Psychological Profile into the Criminal Mind

A Psychological Profile into the Criminal Mind

REX BUTTERFIELD, PH.D.

Copyright © 2004 by Rex Butterfield, Ph.D..

Library of Congress Number: 2004095576
ISBN: Hardcover 1-4134-6493-9
       Softcover 1-4134-6492-0

All rights reserved. No part of this book may be reproduced or transmitted in any form or by any means, electronic or mechanical, including photocopying, recording, or by any information storage and retrieval system, without permission in writing from the copyright owner.

This book was printed in the United States of America.

To order additional copies of this book, contact:
Xlibris Corporation
1-888-795-4274
www.Xlibris.com
Orders@Xlibris.com

Contents

INTRODUCTION 11
ACKNOWLEDGMENTS 17
LETTER FROM THE AUTHOR 19

PART ONE - CRIMINOLOGY 101

CHAPTER ONE :   SOCIAL ENVIRONMENT 25
                Immediate Environment
                Medias
                Conformity
CHAPTER TWO: ATTITUDES 37
                Prejudice, and Stereotypes
                The Theory of Cognitive Dissonance
                Selective Exposure
                Transference
CHAPTER THREE :   BORN TO BE CRIMINALS 46
                The Theory of Cesare Lombraso
                The Theory of Vincent Castillo
                Case File

PART 2 - CRIMINOLOGY 202

CHAPTER FOUR :   FEMALE CRIMINOLOGY 55
                The Rise of Female Crime
                Prostitution

	Physio and P.M.D.
	Employment Causes
	Female Crime Statistics
CHAPTER FIVE :	PEER/GANG PRESSURE 60
	Factors:
	Protection
	Peer Influence
	Family Environment
	Family
	Acceptance
	Gang Statistics
CHAPTER SIX :	CRIMINAL PATTERNS 66
	Rehabilitation
	Modus Operandi
	Profiles
	Patterns:
	Crimes of Opportunity
	First Timers
	Short Term Goals
	Habitual Offenders
	Crimes of Passion

PART 3 - CRIMINOLOGY 303

CHAPTER SEVEN :	CRIME 85
	Murder
	Case File
	Manslaughter
	Vehicular Manslaughter
	Robbery
	Car Jacking

	Sex Offense	
	Drug Offense	
	Assault	
	Kidnapping	
CHAPTER EIGHT :	ILLEGAL SUBSTANCES	97
	Means of Obtaining	
	Drugs: Cause and Effect	
	Alcohol Statistics	
CHAPTER NINE :	PRISON INVOLVEMENT	110
	Drugs in Prison	
	Confinement	
	Breeding Grounds	
	Family Contact	
	Religion	
	Talent	
	Prison Statistics	

PART 4 - CRIMINOLOGY 404

CHAPTER TEN :	STATISTICS	125
	Economic Loss (Chart)	
	UCR	
	Chart of Reported Crimes	
	Gender	
	Race	
	State vs. Federal	
CONCLUSION		133
GLOSSARY		135

OTHER EXCITING BOOKS FROM THIS AUTHOR

In print:
The Official Guide to Interrogation.

Soon to be released: Fiction
The Ultimate Conspiracy

INTRODUCTION

WHEN I FIRST began to write this book, I didn't have any idea as to what route I was going to take. The topic alone is so complex and vast that I didn't think I could have written a book about criminal behavior without any criminology degrees. But fortunately, due to my extensive legal battles with the Criminal Justice System, I was able to use my knowledge and experiences to create something positive out of a negative situation.

Everyday, crime is glorified of every form in the media. It's impossible to escape all the miseries of the world and not be effected by it. This book is targeted at preventing the cycle of misery from continuing.

The first thing we need to do is work to prevent criminal behavior from forming in our immediate environment. If every neighborhood were to work together at crime prevention, this nation would be a safer place to live. It would also reduce the criminal mentality from deep rooting itself in the minds of our youth.

If you take a minute to look at the statistics in chapter ten, you will realize just how much a single crime effects everyone in this nation. This is because every crime carries a hefty price tag with it. Our taxes are effected by each and every crime. At the end of this year, write to congress to get the budget for crime prevention in this nation and you will realize that crime is a very expensive burden on all of us.

I never realized that my very own criminal actions could have effected so many people. My criminal action never really effected me emotionally until I put myself into my victims shoes. The mere fact the I caused someone pain, even if it was only financial pain, was cause enough for me to take a serious look at why I went the criminal route instead of obtaining a legal job to pay the bills. It was not an easy thing to do. Being honest with yourself is very hard, especially when you know that your life isn't all that wonderful. Most people hide their faults in a protective shield, always lying to themselves into believing that their life is flawless. But no one is perfect and everyone has, as they say, skeletons in their closets. I only hope that the people with criminal skeletons become honest with themselves and realize that their actions effect more people than themselves.

It has taken me many months to compile all of the research within this book. I could have written it a lot quicker, but it wouldn't have been fare to my readers. I try to be very thorough and accurate.

Every chapter has significance to the rehabilitation and deterrence of criminal behavior in people. I felt it was very important to examine the causes and effects of emotions that surround deviant behavior. For without emotion, everyone would be void of individual characteristics.

In chapter one, I examine the immediate environment and what impact it has on us as a whole. Societies are built around the emotions of the majority in that area. We depend on our immediate environment to sculpture us into becoming who we are.

Media plays a very important role in our lives, it's what's in the media that effects us as a society.

And finally, conformity. This emotion is easily explained as this; we often agree with peoples opinions even if we don't necessarily believe in them, just for the sake of argument.

In chapter two, I concentrate on one specific emotion: ATTITUDE.

Attitude sculptures us into becoming who we become. Often times, we depend on this emotion as a guidance for acceptance. But, for whatever reasons we allow attitudes to shape us, they will continue to effect us.

In chapter three, I take a look at two theories about criminal behavior and the possibility of heredity playing an important part in it. They are very interesting reads and I figured that I'd share them with you.

I also included a case file from a law book about a crime that was very interesting and somewhat relevant to this chapter. One of the individuals that were convicted of the crime was said to of been born with criminal intentions.

In chapter four, I examine the very controversial subject of female criminals.

I begin with the growing rise into crime amongst females. One crime in particular is prostitution, said to be the oldest profession.

Increasingly, the debate into whether or not a woman's menstrual cycle causes aggressive and possibly criminal behavior is an ongoing subject in the Criminal Justice and the psychological worlds.

Finally, I take a look at criminal statistics for females.

Chapter five, to me, is a very important chapter that deals with how the pressures from the immediate environment and our peers play a very significant role in increasing the possibility of criminal actions. I take a brief look into the five main areas of how peer pressure can influence someone into participating in criminal behavior. These five areas are:

★ Protection
★ Peer Influence
★ Family Environment
★ Family
★ Acceptance

Then I give the reader a brief overview on gang statistics and its impact on society.

In chapter six, I explore the patterns of criminal behavior. Even though I don't get deep into the psychological reasons as to how a person falls into one of these categories, I inform the reader about each pattern.

I begin on explaining what rehabilitation, modus operandi, and profiles are before I explain the different patterns themselves. This gives the reader an opportunity to understand the patterns a little better.

Chapter seven is very interesting for anyone that never knew the difference between different crimes. I felt that since this book is targeted towards the deterrence into criminal behavior, I felt it was a relevant subject to touch on.

Many people assume that an assault is the same thing as a car jacking. Although they are similar in many respects, they differ in most. Or another example is, that a vehicular manslaughter is the same as a murder. These misconceptions confuse people enough.

In chapter eight, I write about illegal substances and the causes and effects it has on the person who consumes it. Illegal substances play an important part in criminal statistics and increase the possibility for someone to commit a crime in order to support their habit.

In chapter nine, I take the reader on a journey into the prison system. The reader learns the inner workings of the prison system from a person that is currently in that environment; me.

The topics are very important as to how prisoners live in an environment that is surrounded with negative behavior. I explain to the reader that prison isn't targeted at rehabilitating inmates. The inmate has to want to become rehabilitated.

At the end of this chapter, I break down the statistics about prison. You will be amazed at the numbers as I was.

And finally chapter ten.

This chapter is to give the reader a look at how serious crime is embedded in our society. These statistics are real and they represent the truth about crime in the United States. Upon reading this chapter, you will be perplexed by how severe this problem with crime really is.

Unfortunately, many in the legal system know the problems and don't know how best to handle it. Without a good plan in youth and rehabilitative programs, how can we expect to rectify this never ending problem. I can only speak for myself and my opinions are just that, my opinions. I hope the reader understands that we as a society needs to address these issues of crime and try to come up with a workable plan to reverse the crime rate.

As I've said, I'm not a criminologist or psychologist by trade but I have the upper hand in those fields because of experience. I hope my experience helps those who read this book and enjoy it as much as I enjoyed writing it.

ACKNOWLEDGMENTS

I WISH TO acknowledge and thank the following people. The importance isn't the order of the list, it's the people, and the contribution they have made in my life.

Above all of my acknowledgments, I'd wish to express my deepest apologies and sympathy to anyone I've ever wronged. I truly apologize. Some good has come out of this bad situation. My life has changed.

To my daughter, Angelica (Jelly), for helping me realize that parenting is a very serious and warm responsibility, and that life has more to offer. You are daddies little girl.

To Belinda, thanks for taking the time out to get to know me for who I am, and love me for who I am. Fate works in mysterious ways.

To my mother, I owe you a lot more than words could ever express. You have always believed in me, and I hope that I'm making you proud of me.

To Xavier for always asking me with his big eyes, "How's the book going?" And for putting a smile on my face. This one's for you, punk.

To both of my brothers, thanks for making me feel like an older bother should and believing in me. Sean and Brendon.

Murray, I hope that you are looking down at me with pride. I will never forget you.

To Wilfredo (Ruiz) Guay, thanks for creating the front cover. Your talents go beyond words.

And above all, Joan. You have been my friend and confidant for many years and pushed me to strive better. Thank you.

LETTER FROM THE AUTHOR

THIS QUEST TO "decode" on how a person's life evolves from childbirth to prison cell began upon my own desire on how and why I began a life of crime. There was no instant revelation, or sudden enlightenment that encouraged me to write this book, only the desire to understand what caused me to commit numerous crimes.

In most books written by criminologists, sociologists, or behavioral scientists that I have read and researched involving the criminals state of mind, and the progressive states that lead to a person's downfall, I've noticed that they all lack key elements about the why not only the how. It is the most important question involving crime.

WHY DO WE COMMIT CRIMES AGAINST MANKIND?

Armed with this burning question, I began to search for the truth. Although I've studied psychology half my life, I've never truly been able to grasp the logic into the criminal acts themselves. I know it may seem odd or even a lie if I were to inform the reader that a very large amount of criminals lack the insight into their acts, but it's true. Many criminals never took a minute to absorb their illegal deed. The reader may assume that once in prison the offender will reflect on their crime and feel remorse. The reason is that most of them feel that they did nothing wrong and that society is to blame for their incarceration.

Throughout my incarceration, I've had countless conversations with my fellow inmates about what led to incarceration, and how if possible their childhood background may have been a factor into their imprisonment. I never imagined that the information that I had obtained from these conversations would help me to not only write this book but also contribute with the assistance of my own rehabilitation. Additionally, it has also strengthened my belief that deviant behavior can be changed. But without a solid plan in sight that is a real solution and not a temporary means to satisfy the public, the Criminal Justice System will continue to be in business. Especially in this day and age where forensic science is putting a damper on criminal activities. No wonder prisons are increasing in population, crime is getting harder to commit. Let's try to prevent crime from happening in the first place the humane way instead of continuously warehousing offenders of the law.

This text isn't a solution to abolishing criminal behavior from the nations streets. This is only a study guide to producing a better insight on a criminal's behavioral pattern. Each criminal is an individual, and each person's background must be investigated thoroughly to pinpoint certain characteristics that may have increased the possibility for his deviancy.

Due to the fact that I have committed crimes, my insight into criminal behavior is far more advanced than most criminologist or scientist can ever compile in their research. They fail to realize that interviewing prisoners and collecting data can only educate them to a minimum, whereas I have intimate knowledge into criminal behavior and as long as I'm honest with myself I can share with you my knowledge. Additionally, prisoners being interviewed will almost always hold back important information. It's a fact. So be cautious when reading other books on criminality.

In writing this book, I tried to examine principal topics that were relevant to the theme so the reader can grasp a better understanding about this serious epidemic that is plaguing our society. This is my opinion, and people may not agree with my research, but if people concentrate on the subject, our world will be a better place to live.

I sincerely hope that this book deters the reader from ever considering violating the law, or cease any behavior that may be questionable in a court of law. Take my experiences and learn from them. It took me a long time to realize that crime is wrong and that inflicting emotional and psychological and physical pain to another human is unjust.

Rex Butterfield, Ph.D

PART ONE
CRIMINOLOGY 101

CHAPTER ONE
SOCIAL ENVIRONMENT

IMMEDIATE ENVIRONMENT

THE PSYCHOLOGICAL MAKEUP that enables someone to commit crimes when they know the difference between right and wrong begins to form at a very early age in life. That's why for many years scientists and psychologists have been working hand to hand to determine if heredity plays an important part in structuring our behavioral patterns throughout our entire genetics, it's a study in which organisms inherit the traits from their parents that forms to help control their behavioral conduct. The most obvious important trait inherited is the structure of the brain, our nervous system. To produce numerous chemicals that are essential to the transmission of nervous impulses and basic daily functions of the brain, and how our glands manufacture chemicals that affect our central nervous system, and most importantly help to regulate our moods and emotional state.

Researchers have found concrete evidence to believe that the inherited genes that structure our body and brain is responsible for numerous aspects in our behavioral states, but one vital question has plagued scientists, and psychologists since the beginning of studying the importance between heredity and behavior, and just how much of an influence does genes have on our emotions?

The question itself is so complex. It literally means do we-as humans- absorb our parent's genes and traits to have a life long effect on our behavior, the ability to comprehend and learn. How much intelligence is passed down, and personalities as a whole? Or, are our genes given to us by our parents; just the raw materials that evolve as we grow that form from our environment, and life experience?

The relative importance between heredity and environment has been the topic of considerable controversy. For example, William James, the most prominent early American psychologist, believed that the vast majority of our behavior is regulated in great extent by power human instincts present at birth. Whereas John Watson, an American psychologist that founded the theory of behaviorism believed that newborns can be conditioned by their existing environments. This seemingly endless debate is often referred to as the nature-nurture controversy.

Most findings support both sides of this debate. For it would be hard pressed to find any psychologist to believe that just one side is correct and not both. The prevailing view is that both nature and nurture play significant roles in the development of behavioral traits. Like heredity seems to set tendencies and limitations. But, the environment takes over to encourage or discourage the development and effect of the newborn and in the progression of his life. The question is not whether, but how much influence do either of them influence such individual aspects of behavior and personality as a way we perceive and interpret the world around us, our intelligence and ability to learn from experiences, our behavioral makeup and emotional state are most importantly, our reactions to stress and problems.

As we grow in age, we get bombarded with numerous emotions that our environment helps us develop. Of course, heredity can cause behavioral traits that we will carry with us for our entire lives. It's our environment that forms our way of emotional thinking and forms who we become. That's not to say that you will become an exact duplicate of your environment, but as research has shown, we will develop many emotional traits that form our environment. Whether those traits promote criminal behavior is on an individual basis.

Prisons are populated with inmates of background similarities and experiences that suggests that they allowed their environment to encourage criminal behavior and that crime is decidedly an occupation for social status and monetary rewards instead of rising above their environment and not engage in any criminal behavior.

In many environments, prison experience is a show of manly strength and a right of passage. It is unfortunate though that we allow negative behavior to encourage action that we would otherwise not absorb if it weren't for peer pressure and environmental encouragement. Without those pressures from our immediate environment our behavioral makeup would change whereas pressure in any form causes stress to impede of own behavioral growth.

There are exceptions where environment causes an immediate stress inducing emotion that may cause you to act out in a violent manner that alters your behavioral state. I will examine in depth the different emotions that cause criminal acts in a later chapter. Because its very important to demonstrate the different emotional states in order to learn how to avoid becoming entrapped, or manipulated by such an emotion. If you can learn the differences and learn to identify the signs of the different emotions it will enable the reader to avoid the pitfalls and traps caused by each emotional state.

Other people are important to us and influence us because human beings are social animals. We require company and help of other humans in need such as food, clothing, shelter, and protection from enemies. We can survive only by establishing some type of society, which is the term applied to any group of people who occupy the same geographical region and cooperate in the same manner of acceptable living.

The society into which we are born begins to influence us almost from the moment of birth. We develop from child to adult not in a vacuum, but in close interaction with our parents, family, teachers, and schoolmates. From all these people, we learn the ways of our own society. We learn the ways of the English language. We learn how Americans speak, behave towards one another, and express, or conceal our emotions. Later we learn what people in our societies believe and what they value. We learn the customs and laws that dictate a whole host of activities finding a mate to forming a business deal. The process is called Socialization.

The way children are integrated into society through the exposure is the actions and opinions of other members of society. In many ways children become products of their own society molded by the customs and rules that make up its culture or established way of life.

The term "culture" embraces all physical objects that make up a society like clothing, shelter, tools, artistic creations, subcultures, etc. The terms also includes:

Societies language
Beliefs
Family Relations
Rules and Laws
Customary Patterns of Behavior

These ingredients can form a very dangerous mixture if society isn't careful enough because every single emotion, and every custom is closely regarded as a pattern for behavior.

Hillary Clinton had once said, "It takes an entire village to raise a child". That statement is very true in most societies. For without constant monitoring on every behavioral wave; that society can become plagued with negative behavior. Look at inner-city areas where crime and criminal behavior is rampant. The average citizen in society is concerned with immediate circles that they become immune to the deterioration of their society as a whole. This unfortunate emotion of self-preservation is sometimes caused by the sometimes-justified fear that involvement may place them into mortal danger.

In the inner-city areas where crime is ramped, pride and drugs cause a huge part of crime. We'll get into drugs later on.

Pride has caused the deaths of many people that may or may not have had any thing to do with the cause for the action. For without this extreme emotion that forces grown men to act in a criminal manner there would be a statistically lower amount of crime and criminal activity. Unfortunately, there is much media that fuel that raw emotion for a society to have a reduced amount of criminal behavior in it.

MEDIAS

Throughout our entire lives, we are bombarded by media from the day we are born until our very last breath. It's impossible to escape most forms of media in this day and age. Now whether media has a significant effect on our emotional upbringing depends on the individual. Researchers suggest that the media does play a role in who we become, its influence is only as strong as the individual's will.

Below, I've listed nine forms of media that surrounds us every waking minute; unless of course you are a recluse.

- ★ Television
- ★ Music
- ★ Video Games
- ★ Movies
- ★ Books
- ★ Magazines
- ★ Radio
- ★ Clothing with Criminal Related Slogans
- ★ Computers

Let's expand on why I believe how media increases an individuals possibility to engage in criminal behavior. I am referring to new areas of criminal and deviant behavior that weren't common and active in our society. These medias may increase a person's knowledge into deviant behavior, but whether or not the individual allows himself to be influenced by a media is on him. These medias are to inform and to abuse the creativity of the creator's mind is on the individual.

Television

Society has begun this perverse obsession with real television and court related shows that target the miseries or problems of other people. Additionally, networks have increased the production of shows that have extreme criminal and violent themes.

Everyone grew up watching cartoons and were entertained with each and every episode. We then allow the tradition to continue with our children, but if you were to actually sit down and absorb the violent content every cartoon has, you would be reluctant to allow your children to view them anymore. Especially at a tender age where easy influence is a strong possibility.

Music

Music is a prime example of how verbal expression can increase the popularity of criminal behavior. Violent and criminally based themes aren't just limited to being expressed and idolized in just type of music. Almost every form of music has been known to increase the popularity of criminal behavior. I'll break down every type of music to demonstrate even minute instances of this type of behavior being expressed through musical lyrics.

Classical and Operas:

Although most operas don't require translations to understand how much violence and criminal activity there are included into them, it's evident that when Shakespeare and Puccini scripted works that became sensational hits, the violent themes and plots weren't intended as a selling point.

In many symphonies, classical music tells a tale of tragic circumstances through their music.

Rap and Hip Hop:

Since the beginning rap was introduced to the public in 1979, it has grown from being popular in the urban communities to becoming a dominant record selling force that spans the globe.

But . . .

The criminal and negative behavior glorified in the songs are, for the most part, the main theme of every song. True, not every song targets criminal behavior, but it is the most popular subject. Every type of crime is glorified and described in full detail. The reason for glorifying crime is because it's a huge selling point. Many criminals can relate to the main topics and that can possibly intensify bolder acts of crime.

There have been Congressional hearings as to rap lyrics that are extremely violent and disrespect the laws of nature. The outcome usually entails stricter labeling laws on the album covers detailing any questionable lyrics.

Rock and Heavy Metal:

Many bands in Heavy Metal music promote sadistic and satanic worship. Although most bands that use satanic themes in their music don't actually practice the religion themselves, many teenagers believe that devil and evil worship can bring them closer to the music.

Many kids have actually blamed the music as a cause for their criminal actions, stating that the music influenced them to commit crimes. In one particular incident, a teenager alleges that upon listening to a heavy metal band, he was so influenced by the music that he murdered both of his parents as a satanic sacrificial ceremony.

Country Music:

Country music has always been one of the popular music styles in America for a very long time and will continue to be a dominant force in the music industry.

But . . .

This popularity hasn't reduced the often-criminal themes in their lyrics. Often times, you will hear an artist sing of the following subjects that violate numerous humanitarian laws.

* Gun violence
* Outlaw situations
* The hanging death of rivals
* multiple gun homicides

R&B, Soul, and Slow music:

Many readers will initially balk at the idea that illegal activities can be found in love related music, but that's because it is so embedded into our society that we except the fact that this type of behavior is expressed.

Listen to your favorite heart break song and you may hear of acts of revenge to destroy personal property like a house, a car, or getting someone fired from their job.

Although we don't tend to realize what types of topics are expressed in our favorite music, it's evident that many songs, from most types of music, contain criminally related themes. I am a lover of all types of music and am in no way saying that music is a factor in promoting deviant behavior. I'm merely trying to encourage the reader to take into account the different ways we accept this type of behavior to be included into our daily lives.

Video Games

When we think of video games we envision entertainment and a fun challenge. But some video games are extremely violent and encourage the player to partake in creating violent situations.

Numerous times I've heard children express their desire to kill a character in the game. To me, that sounds extremely disturbing.

Video games have become so controversial that parents went to Congress to protest the continued manufacturing of these games. Congress in response, enforced video game manufactures to label all video game cartridges with warning labels of the games violent contents. Unfortunately, this doesn't deter kids from obtaining these cartridges nor do they deter some parents from purchasing them for their children.

Below, I felt it was important to list the several themes that are in many games. They aren't in every game, mind you, but I figured they were worth mentioning.

- ★ Drug use
- ★ Weapon use
- ★ Criminal related themes
- ★ Sexual situations
- ★ Gory details

Movies

Since movies are the highest monetary grossing medias there are, movie studios try to push the envelop of how outlandish they can get away with. Movies that glamorize criminal behavior, in every magnitude, often have unrealistic themes but are seen as entertaining to the public. What's disturbing is the fact that the Government restricts the amount of sexual content in movies, but allows movie studios to promote extreme violence in every conceivable way.

To define my above statement in simpler terms, I'll say it like this:

The government permits movie studios to market a movie about a homicidal maniac, savagely killing numerous people, but enforces, in a legal manner, to restrict movie studios to film a breast being caressed without extreme warning labels. This tells the movie viewer that violence is acceptable, but intimate sexual contact between two consenting adults is wrong. I'm not saying that sex should be promoted to young adults, just think about what's considered acceptable in our society.

Books

This media has been including criminal behavior since written words were first created as a form of expression. To give you an example of how long abnormal behavior has been written, read anything by Shakespeare and you will read an extreme amount of violence.

William Shakespeare was a poet and a dramatist from 1564 to 1616, and in that era violence was a way that monarchs and governments controlled their citizens. Maybe he was a product of his time and violent behavior was looked upon as just and a means of surviving, but what about our authors now? Makes you wonder about the excuses used now to promote novels that contain violent and criminal behavior. I shouldn't be one to talk, because I'm not immune for such past works.

Magazines

With such a wide variety of magazines in print, many publishers try to create new ideas that grab the interests of the public with almost illegal behavior. The topics may range from encouraging drug paraphernalia to extreme violence to sexual perversion. With more and more publishers pushing the envelop with criminal subjects, the variety of topics are becoming more outrageous.

There are magazines that demonstrate how the readers can construct dangerous weapons, or how to perform very devious pranks that could possibly inflict physical harm. This in turn can cause the one that was pranked to avenge that action.

Radio

Aside from music, radio stations have been encouraging their DJ's to perform outrageous pranks onto it's listeners or unsuspecting guests. They also hold discussions that favor extreme violence, sexual content, or other subjects laced with criminal behavior. What's more disturbing is that children of any age can listen to any radio station without restrictions. No parent can constantly keep their child from listening to the radio everyday.

Apparel

It's ironic how offensive with derogatory language, or phrases are banned from television, but it's perfectly legal to express the following on clothing:

* Hatred
* Drug use
* Violence
* Sexual innuendos
* Criminal situations

I've actually seen someone wearing a tee-shirt that illustrated a baby of color hanging from a tree. Fortunately for me and that individual, I was in a car and couldn't stop. I might have gotten into trouble.

Tee-shirts often have in bold eye-catching letters very offensive sayings on them to increase drawing attention. At least with a book, television, or movies, you have the ability to not be offended by their contents by simply not looking at them. Whereas, apparel with offensive sayings and/or graphics, you are being forced to view the wearers opinions.

Computers

With technology enabling medias to reach practically anyone on earth with the use of a computer, criminal and deviant subjects are just a click away. The information highway is practically unrestricted. The user can learn anything. From receiving a college degree to learning how to construct a bomb can be found. Can you imagine the enormity of web-sites that cater to criminal activities? There are also hate groups and organizations that promote their beliefs onto the public in hopes of attracting more members.

I didn't give the above examples as an excuse for crime. I'm merely informing my readers that criminal glorification is everywhere, including the media.

If someone was influenced by a media into committing a crime then that individual should be dealt with according to the law. A psychological evaluation should be conducted to see why that individual was so influenced by a media to commit a crime.

Unfortunately, many medias receive bad publicity due to people that committed a crime and blamed the media for their actions.

Don't get me wrong, I'm an avid fan of our constitution indicating that freedom of speech is our right. I also don't believe that we shouldn't necessarily blame medias for entertaining the public, they should just take into consideration the type of subjects they inform the public on.

Now-a-days, instructional books print in bold caption, "For informational purposes only", this is to prevent the reader from blaming the book for any of their actions. Maybe movies, television, and music should put that label on their products also?

The more uncertain we are of where we stand in society and how we should act, the more likely we are to rely on the behavior of those around us and make comparisons. For example, if you go to a party that caters to the Communist party, how can you fit in without first seeing how others are socializing?

The theory of social comparisons also holds that our search for guidance strongly influences our self-esteem; indeed our entire self-image. We tend to self-judge our abilities and our worth with those around us.

The theory maintains mostly in our comparisons with other people in either our society, or even total strangers. We cannot state for sure – as a proven fact – that we are good students, good athletes, or good at anything, for that matter, unless we compare ourselves with other people that are considered good in that field. We have to try to decide how we rack in comparison with other people.

The opinions of other people play a far greater role in self-esteem than could be imagined by a person who has had limited exposure to social environments and its emphasis on social influences.

Sometimes, it should be added, we merely pay lip service to the opinions and ideas expressed by others; thus engaging in what social psychologists call Expedient Conformity. For example, a woman who strongly favors the democratic candidate in a common election may find herself at a party where everyone else is enthusiastic about the Republican Party. She may conform and go along with the others, even though she is convinced that they are wrong, just to avoid any arguments and win acceptance.

CHAPTER TWO
ATTITUDES

IT SEEMS ONLY appropriate that an entire chapter be dedicated to one specific emotion. This emotion has the ability to change a criminal's behavior in an instant or over time. This depends on how strong the emotion is at the time and how much effect it has on the individual. This emotion is attitude. For without an attitude, we wouldn't have the ability to be individuals; our likes or dislikes wouldn't exist.

This chapter may be a little technical in psychological terms, but the importance to fully understand this emotion is invaluable. This will help you to understand the criminal mentality, because people become criminals due to their emotional state about the economy, social values, and any other topic that can drive a person to commit crimes. Just have an open mind when studying this chapter.

All of us, as we grow up, acquire many strong beliefs and feelings, or what psychologists call attitudes. These attitudes are towards people and emotional situations. In addition, we are favorable and unfavorable towards members of various:

Ethnic Groups	Authority Figures
Foreigners	Teachers

Rich People   Friends
Poor People   unions

When it comes to politics and the nation's government, many people have strong attitudes. Whether they are positive or negative, people also have attitudes about:

National Defense   Crime
Taxation   Religions
Welfare   Relatives
Budget   Human Rights

★ And every other issues and institution that make up our society as a whole.

Attitudes are not just mere "off the cuff" judgements that are made casually and can easily be changed. Instead they're deeply ingrained; as if constituting a basic part of our personality. We acquire many of them through the process of socialization, and they tend to influence most of us throughout our entire lives.

In a crime infested society, many children are forced, from an early age, into committing criminal acts. Or they are encouraged into joining a gang simply as a means to staying alive. These are the same children that if raised in a different environment, the majority of them would grow up to lead productive lives and respect the laws of humanity.

It's truly unfortunate that their environment and the pressures from their peers increase the chances of them engaging in criminal behavior. This is simply a form of survival. You may read this and be somewhat skeptical, but truth be told, many inner city children are faced with decisions on whether or not to engage in criminal behavior. Many of these children are so young that they may not understand the difference between right and wrong. Many of these children were raised in a family environment that is contaminated with criminal behavior. So, the child is growing up thinking that laws are meant to be broken. This is extremely stressful on the child, especially when he learns later on in life that criminal behavior is illegal. This confuses the child further.

Of course, there are instances were the child overcomes the peer and family pressure and become a law abiding citizens, but they are far and few between.

OUR NEED FOR GUIDANCE

Another reason for conformity is that we need the help of other people in developing an accurate view of our physical and social environment. We cannot get through life successfully and may not even survive unless we understand the world around us.

To cite some extreme examples why we, as humans, need guidance growing up, read on.

"You can get yourself killed if you venture out to sea in a boat at a time when a more experienced seaman would know a storm is coming."

Or let's say that you're about to eat a wild berry that an expert would know that the berry contains poisons.

In dealing with other people, you can come to grief if you misjudge the reactions of an armed robber with a show of resistance. Or on a more common level, you may lose your job if you fail to realize your employers desire for promptness and a strict dress code. There are many instances, everyday, in which we interact with others and learn from them. This interaction enables us to understand ourselves better and that in turn enables us to deal with living in that society.

It's not uncommon to mimic the mannerisms of those we interact with most. This is especially true if you look up to that individual. This behavior is often the reason that children need to be sheltered from negative behavior.

The need for guidance to behave in an acceptable manner in society is an important psychological concept called, "The Theory of Social Comparison." The theory holds that we usually have no objective, or scientific way to evaluate our abilities, opinions, or the propriety of our actions. Therefore, we can only judge ourselves by comparing ourselves with others and by comparing ourselves with others in our environment; usually our friends or other people. We believe that we are normal, but sometimes we seem strange to whom we happen to socialize with.

With the population of the world rising every year, environments are becoming bombarded with a multitude of cultures. This is because people from one nation migrates to another. This forms a subculture in an already existent culture.

Within our society, there exists many subcultures, or ways of life that differ from one another in many important respects. Some of these subcultures exist partly because this nation has been settled over by people from different parts of the world, bringing with them their own particular customs and values.

Then you have subcultures that are religiously based. Still other cultures depend on the occupational and social status.

All in all, America is a mixture of race, politics, sexual preference, military factions, and life styles in general.

Whatever the customs and rules may be, every culture and subculture molds its children accordingly. Especially in a culture as complex as ours, not every child will be socialized to follow the same customs and rules.

Socialization is a universal process and learning experience. It is a form of learning that gives a person a more pervasive and lasting effect than anything learned in school, (although schools also serves to socialize its students). In one way or another, socialization gives us all a life long tendency to think and act like the people with whom we grow up with.

There are of course rebels that resist the influence of socialization and break the laws within that society. Some of them become criminals at war with society. Then on the flip side, you have the other half that become innovators. They sometimes re-shape history by jolting society out of its old ways and into new ones.

Despite the exceptions, however, most people follow the rules and customs in their society and behave accordingly. Social psychologists have discovered through years of research, that most human beings display strong tendencies towards obedience, or submissions to authority.

Conformity plays a very significant role in who we become. Whether it's the tendency to go to outrageous lengths under peer pressure or make us behave in an unexpected way. This emotion is so powerful that it can cause us to act other than our normal way.

OUR DEPENDENCE ON APPROVAL

One reason seems to be that we depend on people for many of our psychological satisfactions. It's a pleasant feeling to win the approval as an accepted member of your group of peers. However, it is highly unpleasant to be rejected by the group and perhaps even be subject to ridicule. It can be very difficult to stand alone and sometimes dangerous in a society where proving yourself is often required. These societies often force children to join criminal gangs as a means of protection and is many times enforced to demonstrate loyalty and the continuance of protection.

Now, not only does their membership possibly force them to commit criminal acts and possibly violent deeds, but now they become an extremely vulnerable target for the other gangs.

Attitudes within our social environment have an impact on who we become and what we believe growing up. It is these attitudes that can increase an individuals risk into criminal behavior if he/she allows their surroundings to influence them into such an attitude.

It is chiefly this "for" or "against" quality that distinguishes attitudes from more superficial to less influential opinions. That's why psychologists have invested considerable time trying to determine how people acquire them, cling to them, but sometimes change them.

Attitudes are not necessarily based on evidence. Some of them simply represent the effects on socialization and conformity to the social environment we are in. Our ingenuity at finding ways to maintain our attitudes despite strong opposition arguments seems almost boundless.

There are two main attitudes that seem to reflect who we are and who we become throughout our lives. These attitudes conjure up strong emotions that can shape who we become even if there are no concrete evidence to support facts.

These two attitudes are:

Prejudice:

A prejudice is an attitude that an individual maintains stubbornly as to be virtually immune to any information, or experience that would disprove your reasons for that attitude. In our society, prejudice often causes minorities from obtaining employment in a certain establishment.

Stereotype:
A stereotype is an attitude held by a large number of people that disregards individuals beliefs and differences and holds that all members of a certain group behave in the same manner. People are making judgements on the basis of stereotypes when they claim that all women are flighty and that all men are chauvinists.

Prejudice and Stereotypes affect many forms of human behavior. Even scientists and psychologists are not immune from becoming influenced and may determine that a judgement by their colleagues is correct simply by the fact that the majority deems it correct. The best trained scientists and psychologists sometimes become so enamored of a particular theory that they refuse to abandon it even in the face of mounting evidence. Even in personal relationships, they may judge new acquaintants on the basis of stereotypes that make them suspicious of certain kinds of people who might prove highly congenial if only given a chance.

One reason attitudes change is that socialization process continues throughout life. In our early years, our parents are the primary instruments of socialization and we tend to adopt their attitudes as our own.

Our attitudes can be compared to a house that undergoes frequent remolding, expansion, and painting over the years. In some ways the house never changes, yet it is never really the same.

What kind of new experiences and new information are likely to produce attitude changes throughout our lives? One answer comes from proponents of what is called:

THE THEORY OF COGNITIVE DISSONANCE

This theory maintains that we have a strong urge to be consistent and rational in our thinking. We also need to preserve agreement and harmony among our beliefs, feelings, and behavior, therefore preserve our attitudes.

When consistency and harmony are broken, we experience cognitive dissonance: We may manage to tolerate the inconsistency, but cognitive dissonance tends to be highly uncomfortable, and we may be strongly motivated to restore harmony by making some kind of adjustment.

In some cases, new factual information is enough to create cognitive dissonance and bring about attitude. For example, many people that were once opposed to birth control have been greatly influenced. This is because new factual information, that has appeared in recent years, about the population explosion and the dangers of worldwide overcrowding. They once had the cognitive belief that populating the world is a good thing. This cognitive belief has now changed, and their attitude about birth control has now changed.

Events that have a strong emotional impact may also create an inconsistency that calls for change. For example, imagine if a man who had always regarded women as second class citizens finds himself in love with a woman who is a feminist.

Now onto how attitudes change behavior and how its change can deteriorate an entire society. Even miniscule changes in a social environment has a lasting effect. Whereas, in environments with little change maintain its consistency in the same social pattern.

It seems logical that a change in an attitude, caused by new beliefs or new emotional responses, should cause a change in behavior. Yet, strangely enough, the sequence in events is often exactly the opposite. In many cases, the changes in behavior creates the change in attitude.

Many studies have shown that experimental manipulation of behavior can produce remarkable results. An experiment was conducted with college students that favored the legalization of marijuana. They were told to write an essay describing why and how marijuana should be legalized. But once the essays were written, so did the attitudes of the students' change.

In our everyday lives, new social situations often pushes us in the direction of changes in behavior, and these in turn often lead to changes in attitudes. This has been especially noticeable in recent years in the attitude of whites towards blacks and of blacks towards whites. In general, it has been found that people who have attended school or worked with members of the other race hold more favorable attitudes. While those who have had no interracial contacts tend to feel less favorable. Undoubtedly, the explanation is that new forms of behavior are created because of interacting with other races. Like studying with them, working with them, and treating them as friendly companions have produced new attitude changes.

One type of behavior likely to produce attitude change is the mere act of making a decision. Once we decide to make a decision, that change reflects on our attitude. For every decision, there's a new attitude formed. The realization that your new decision is beneficial towards your emotional state can make decisions develop into a new attitudes.

Up until now, the topic has been limited to the attitude changes that occur as a result to our own experiences, but all of us are under consistent pressure from our environment. Just look at advertisements in your local newspaper, on busses, and taxis. They all try to get you to create a favorable attitude towards their product.

Many organizations work very hard to win support for their causes with very moving advertisements. But their attempt to change to influence the attitudes of large numbers of people faces many obstacles.

It has been found that the audience likely to watch or read any appeal for attitude change is determined largely by a factor called selective exposure. This means that, by and large, persuasive communications reach and appeal to people who are already persuaded. That is to say that since we already tend to associate with subjects we find interesting, our exposure will be limited to specific subjects. For instance, examine your own interest patterns and how it effects your attitude.

The majority of an audience that attends a concert will have a favorable attitude towards that style of music may cause them to vary their preferred band.

This is called Transference.

Transference occurs when you may like one specific brand of toothpaste because you like the dental benefits that your current brand contains. But, then you see a similar brand that contains the same dental benefits as your preferred brand. This brand may contain a new ingredient that your current brand lacks so you switch brands and decide to continue using the new brand.

This same transference occurs in the criminal's mind when one crime seems more appealing now than another. Many factors may play a role in the criminal's mind to decide that his current "occupation" isn't profitable enough for him to maintain his life style, or the crime is becoming too dangerous to continue, or the risks of getting arrested are just too probable. Without these factors, the criminal would continue to commit the same crime over and over because, after all, humans are habitual creatures.

In the criminal's mind, getting away with the act causes the criminal to adopt certain attitudes that may attribute to the continuance of committing the crime. Unfortunately, this attitude may cause the criminal to become bolder with each criminal act and probably increase the criminal to increase the acts themselves. With each act, the criminal becomes bolder and more creative, devising new ways to commit and get away with each crime.

The reason for examining attitudes is simple: "They reflect on the current state of mind" the individual is in that committed the act.

Attitudes also shape the way we perceive our current environment and our everyday actions. They fuel our emotions, and behavior, and sculpture us into becoming who we are. For without attitudes, we would cease to exist as individuals and lack the emotional ability to become who we already are today.

In chapter six, I will explain the certain types of criminal patterns. These are the (MO) Modus Operandis of criminals.

The reason each criminal decides to break the law varies. Many factors that increase the individual to commit crimes include the individual's upbringing, his current social environment, and his current state of mind. Even though the reasons for committing a crime have a basic pattern, we cannot predict why a person decides to commit a crime. We can learn a lot in examining the persons background but no one can pinpoint one single event in that person's life that can be labeled as the factor into committing a crime.

CHAPTER THREE
BORN TO BE CRIMINALS

CESARE LOMBROSO (1836-1909)

A PHYSICIAN NAMED Cesare Lombroso (1836-1909), theorized that he discovered biological proof as to why people become criminals. He believed that everyone who commits a criminal act is born with personality flaws that automatically stimulates deviant behavior and have the inability to curve the urge from preventing their actions from occurring.

His theory was that he found key to understanding criminal behavior through human evolution. After years of gathering systematic data, observation, the measurement of the physical structure of incarcerated inmates, and other relevant information, he concluded that people who committed the most violent criminals were born to commit those acts. His belief was that people that committed crimes were biologically flawed and reproduced animalistic instincts from their primitive ancestors.

His belief was born that criminals were unable to resist violent and criminal urges. Unfortunately, he warned that very little could be done to cure a criminal that was born with the biological characteristics, and only imprisonment can ensure that society is safe from them.

Ironically though, that didn't prevent him from advising prison officials to treat prisoners with this biological flaw as dignified and humanly as possible. He informed them that the criminals were not at fault because their crimes were caused by a biological defect.

Years later, Lombroso's theory was proven wrong by a team of psychologists whom tested and analyzed his theory from every angle. What Lombroso failed to study were the criminals that were never caught and living in society. His theory was only limited to convicted criminals because he theorized that all criminals were caught, which of course is wrong.

For seventy years, psychologists and criminologists knew that Lombroso's theory to be incorrect, but withheld that information from the public because of the possibility that human biology may be a factor, not the cause, in a person's deviant behavior.

Scientists did discover that a part of aggressive behavior can be linked to heredity, meaning that the genes of parents with aggressive behavior can pass that behavior onto their children. That does not mean that this is the cause for any illegal action the child commits.

VINCENT CASTILLO (1932-1988)

A South American scientist/psychologist named Vincent Castillo (1932-1988), conducted a study on heredity and aggressive behavior. He adopted a newborn child from a woman that was sentenced to prison for 15 years. She was convicted of the aggregated murder of her husband.

His initial intention was to raise the child for the woman and give the child a productive environment to grow up in. Otherwise, the child would have gone to the orphanage that was overcrowded and poorly run.

From a very early age, Dr. Castillo observed aggressive behavior in the child, but wasn't sure of the cause. His initial thought was that all kids suffer from the "terrible twos" and this behavior would soon pass. But, by age four his adopted son's aggressive behavior began to increase. It wasn't the environment that ignited the child's behavior because Dr.

Castillo was home schooling him. His interaction with other children was minimal and Dr. Castillo never displayed any aggressive behavior towards his son. Nor could his son have mimicked the behavior from someone else. So he began to study the child and note what, if any cause, could trigger the child's aggressive behavior. He also monitored how often the child got angry.

During a four year period, he kept a journal of his son's activities and noted any severe behavioral problems. He wanted to be certain that his observations weren't biased, so he obtained funding from the government. He then employed two other psychologists and opened up an orphanage for eight children whose mother's were incarcerated for extremely violent offences.

As the years passed, Dr. Castillo and his two colleagues collected data, observing that out of eight children, six displayed aggressive behavior. They also observed every single aspect of their lives and tried to pinpoint what triggers their behavior. They observed that even the most trivial of incidents caused outbursts.

Even after Dr. Castillo published his studies and informed the psychology community on his studies, he and his colleagues continued their studies. Years later, psychologists and scientists agree that an aggressive trait can be biologically passed onto the child. They also concluded that just because a child receives a gene from their parents does not automatically mean that the child will exhibit any traits from that gene.

Lastly, keep in mind that even if there is a small genetic predisposition to commit a crime, there are many more factors that make up criminals to commit criminal acts. Most acts must be learned, as in all human behaviors.

CASE FILE

Just before noon on October 7, 1997, Newark police officer David Figuroa and his partner found Adam Watkins in the fourteenth floor stairwell of Brick Towers, a Newark apartment building. He was badly bruised and, except for a pair of socks, naked. There were no witnesses to what had happened to him. About an hour later, Watkins was pronounced dead at the hospital.

Watkins had been homeless in the days before his death, due to martial difficulties, and had been spending nights at the Brick Towers apartment where Terrell lived with his family (Sherron was staying with his girlfriend in another apartment in that same building). Early on the morning of October 7, 1997, Watkins left the Savage apartment and went to the home of Rashon Baskerville (Baskerville). He arrived there at approximately 8:00 a.m. and fell asleep on the couch.

That same morning, Terrell discovered that a diamond ring, which he believed to be worth $12,000, was missing from his apartment. Shortly after 8:00 a.m., Terrell called and asked Sherron to help research the apartment for the ring. They did not find the ring and, because Terrell suspected that Watkins had stolen the ring, he asked Sherron to take a ride with him to pick up Watkins. The two drove to Baskerville's house. Terrell entered the house while Sherron waited in the car. A few minutes later, Terrell walked out of the house accompanied by Watkins.

After picking up Watkins at Baskerville's house, Terrell drove to see Kenneth Long (Long), the owner of Kenyor Auto Body. Long testified that Watkins "was sitting like he wanted to jump out of the car or something." Terrell told Long that Watkins had been at his home and that his ring was missing. Terrell also told Long that if Watkins took the ring, he was "going to beat him up."

Terrell then drove back to Baskerville's house. According to a written statement given to police by Baskerville, most of which he denied making or could not recall at trial, Terrell told Baskerville "that nigger crossed me," referring to the fact that he allowed Watkins to stay at his home and that Watkins had apparently stolen his diamond ring. When Baskerville asked about Watkins, Terrell told him that Watkins was in his car. Baskerville went outside and observed Watkins sitting in the back seat and Sherron in the front passenger seat.

At some point, Watkins told Baskerville that Terrell's ring was inside the house. When Baskerville said that Watkins could retrieve the ring, Terrell said that Watkins could not get out of the car. Nevertheless, Baskerville, without objection from Terrell, opened the car door for

Watkins. Watkins stepped out of the car and entered the house with Terrell and Baskerville. While in the house, Watkins retrieved the ring and returned it to Terrell and got back into the car. Terrell then drove off with Watkins and Sheron.

Around noon, Terrell called Baskerville and told him, "that cat ain't breathing" (apparently referring to Watkins). According to Baskerville's statement, Terrell asked Baskerville to meet him at Long's auto body shop because, by that time, Watkin's body had been found and there was a large police presence at Terrell's apartment building. Shortly after that call, however, Terrell came to Baskerville's house and said, "[Y]o, man, I don't think that cat was breathing: I hope he ain't dead." Terrell then asked Baskerville to go to the hospital and check on Watkins. Terrell left after Baskerville refused to go to the hospital or to become involved in any way. Subsequently, Baskerville went to the hospital with Alston to find out Watkin's condition. At that time, Baskerville learned that Watkins had been beaten to death.

Around 7:30 p.m., Terrell returned to Long's auto body shop and admitted to Long that "we beat him up" and that Watkins was probably dead. Terrell told Long that if the police questioned him, he should tell them that Terrell was with him at the shop.

Around 8:30 or 9:00 p.m., Terrell drove to Baskerville's house where he learned about Watkins was, if fact, dead. Upon learning of Watkin's death, Terrell began to cry and asked Baskerville what charges could be brought against him. When Baskerville inquired how the assault took place, Terrell stated that "he and [Watkins] were fighting and his brother and his fiends bone rushed him" and Terrell could not stop it. Terrell also told Baskerville that he and Sherron removed Watkins' cloths to humiliate Watkins and to teach him a lesson.

Both Baskerville and Long cooperated with the police investigation. Based on their statements to police, Terrell was indicted first and Sherron was later charged. At trial, the medical examiner, Leonard Sartski, M.D., testified that the cause of Watkins' death was homicide-blunt force trauma to the head and that the other injuries Watkins sustained were "superficial".

Sherron's testimony at trial was similar to Baskerville's statement. He stated that he had agreed to help Terrell search for the ring. After they were unable to locate it, Sherron went to the store to purchase cigarettes. On his return, Terrell asked Sherron to take a ride with him to get Watkins. When the brothers arrived at Baskerville's home, Sherron remained in the car listening to the radio while Terrell went inside. Terrell came out of the house with Watkins, who entered the car of his own violation. Sherron had no recollection of going to Long's auto body business. According to him, while driving away from Baskerville's house, Watkins told Terrell that the ring was at the house. Sherron further testified that, after they retrieved the ring, Watkins reentered the car voluntarily.

According to Sherron, the three men returned to Terrell's apartment building so that Terrell "could beat [Watkins] . . . for stealing out of the house after he gave him somewhere to stay." Sherron testified that Terrell's intention was "[t]o teach a lesson, to teach [Watkins] not to steal from him. Not to kill Adam, just to beat him up." During the fifteen to twenty minute ride back to the apartment building, Sherron testified that Terrell spoke with Watkins about the disappearance of the ring and said to Watkins, "How could you do this to me, you know, man, you know, take from me after I done so much for you?" When the three men arrived at the apartment complex, they walked past a number of people and a security guard. Terrell and Watkins continued to apologize for taking it.

Sherron testified that, when the three men entered the elevator to the brothers' apartment building. Terrell punched Watkins in the face. The elevator door opened on the sixteenth floor and Terrell and Watkins fell out of the elevator. Terrell hit Watkins in the face five or six times, causing him to fall to the ground. Sherron admitted that he kicked Watkins in his side once, when Watkins tried to get up from the floor. (In his statement to the police that was referred to at trial, Sherron stated that he delivered "kicks" to Watkins' side.) More specifically, Sherron testified that, when Watkins attempted to get up on his hands and knees he "kicked him on his side" because he "thought he was going to get up and rush – I thought he was trying to get up to come at my brother." Sherron admitted that he was "mad" at Watkins for stealing from his mother's home but said that he kicked Watkins because he did not want him to be in a position to attack Terrell. Sherron told

Terrell to stop hitting Watkins because "you done proved your point to him, you taught him a lesson." According to Sherron, the brothers left Watkins sitting on the floor, fully clothed. After leaving the building, Sherron testified that he had no idea where Terrell went.

Based on the foregoing evidence, a jury convicted Sherron on all counts. At sentencing, the trial court merged the conspiracy conviction into the kidnapping conviction and the felony murder conviction into murder. The court then sentenced Sherron to a custodial term of life in prison for murder, with an eighty-five percent period of parole ineligibility pursuant to the No Early Release Act (NERA) and to a concurrent thirty-year term of imprisonment with a twenty-five and one-half year period of parole ineligibility pursuant to NERA, for first-degree kidnapping.

Defendant Sherron Savage and his brother, co-defendant Terrell Savage (Terrell), were charged by indictment with second-degree conspiracy to commit kidnapping and/or murder, in violation *left out (Count One); first-degree kidnapping, in violation of *left out (Count Two); first-degree purposeful or knowing murder, in violation of *left out (Count Three); and first-degree felony murder, in violation of *left out (Count Four). In Count Five, Terrell alone was charged with witness tampering, in violation of *left out. Terrell pled guilty to aggravated manslaughter and was sentenced to a thirty-year custodial term with an 85% period of parole ineligibility.

PART 2
CRIMINOLOGY 202

CHAPTER FOUR
FEMALE CRIMINOLOGY

THE RISE OF FEMALE CRIME

WITHIN THE LAST two decades, this country has seen an increase in the development of female involvement in criminal activity. This involvement tends to be the result of a new liberation and independency that has exploded within the female population.

This increase is the result of women committing crimes without the aid of a man as an encouragement because until the last two decades, women's involvement in crime, excluding minor offences, were the result of a male encouraging a female to participate in criminal activity with them or commit acts of crime alone. This is not to say that acts of more severe crimes weren't committed solely as the result of a woman's decision. I am merely saying that the females' involvement within the last two decades has increased.

Before and during these past two decades, the most severe crimes to be committed by female involved crimes of passion and crimes that were drug related. It's evident as to why the statistics in female involvement in criminal activity related with drugs can cause this increase and with the increase of domestic violence. It's evident as to why crimes of passion are on the rise. That's one reason why domestic violence has been activated into a law. In some states, the police can arrest a man or a woman on a domestic violence charge if they feel reasonable cause that one party struck another. To take it a step further, even if one party spit on another it is considered an assault. It's sad to say that some spouses use this law to their own advantage and instead of going through the proper channels to obtain a divorce, they accuse their spouse of domestic violence to ensure they benefit from the arrest.

Due to the dramatic increase in equal opportunity in the work force, the pattern of white-collar crimes has increased within the female statistics. Women have become a strength in Corporate America and have risen up in the corporate ranks as a force to be reckon with.

Along that rise, opportunity for white collar crime has also given women ample opportunity to commit these types of crimes. Unfortunately, due to low amounts of arrests involving this type of crime, the percentages are still relatively low as opposed to males.

Statistically, males continue to dominate female in drug related offenses, but there is a five percent narrowing of the relative gap, and there is a change in this category on the total numbers of arrests that is far greater for females than for males.

Many times, however; these statistics are distorted by the fact that many females, from other countries, are apprehended trying to smuggle illegal drugs into this country for hopes of a better life, or as a means to buy a citizenship. This data should be separate from the drug related arrests involving females within this country, but it's not.

One of the most common crimes committed by females are sexually related. Prostitution is said to be the oldest profession known to man. The power of a woman is so powerful and enticing, that's why that form of criminal behavior is extremely high.

Due to the rise in sexually transmitted diseases and public awareness, the police had to enforce a major crack down. This is due to the explosion in Aids and other sexually related diseases.

Some states have enacted a law making it a felony crime for a prostitute to have HIV, or AIDS and solicit anyone for a sexual act in exchange for anything of value. A prostitute can legally be charged with attempted murder and receive a stiff sentence.

Prostitution will continue to dominate the criminal statistics for females as the number one crime. The only thing required for a female to decide that she wants to prostitute herself is will and opportunity. What drives a woman to commit these types of crimes?

With the female crime rate on the rise in almost every state, only systematic efforts to explain female criminality was available until recently, and it was when criminologists realized that the increase in female related crimes have become, as one criminologist put it, an "epidemic" has occurred. Personally, I think that response is a sexist reply to an increasing problem. To a large extent, our collected theories on female criminals were solely based on common sense interpretations with some statistic data to analyze this increase. Early pre-scientific explanations viewed the female offender as having been corrupted or led astray by a man, but as we now that is not true for a large portion of the statistics.

Another unproven theory about why females commit crimes was when scientists theorized that a woman's menstrual cycle was an important factor. Multiple tests were conducted on this theory with mixed results. Once they concurred that although mood swings and emotions were increased during the menstrual period, they only accounted for certain amount of crimes being committed and even then the evidence was "tainted"; no pun intended.

The hormonal release increases a woman's aggressiveness to certain levels, but only in women who suffer from PMDD (Premenstrual Dysphoric Disorder), was the increase at very aggressive levels. Many females that suffer from PMDD experience severe mood swings and uncontrollable emotional reactions that often result in the suffer lashing out at people for minor, or even no reasons at all.

To demonstrate how early researchers conducted inadequate data gathering and came to incorrect theories, let's look at another theory that turned out to be incorrect. It was assumed that defective intelligence was casually related to crime among both sexes. But that didn't prevent researches from labeling females as the worst culprits. Some of the early research showed that female offenders were below average in intelligence when compared to females with no criminal history.

There are scores of females that took an IQ test and scored low in most subjects. Furthermore, it is plausible that these lower scores result because the samples on intelligence were limited to apprehended offenders who may be disproportionately less gifted than their unapproched counterparts.

Another incorrect theory on the psychological explanation into female crimes are, to a large extent, constitutionally based, because many psychologists that are Sigmond Freud fans view female behavior and personality as anatomically centered. That is to say, they subscribe to the theory of anatomy as the female's destiny and position. Women were seen as anatomically inferior was tooted in their sex organs. These genital deficiencies were the source of such problems as penis envy, masochism, narcissism, exhibitionism, and are the driving force behind a woman's desire to become a man. Evidently, these theories were created amongst sexist men and their inability to analyze the true underlying problem.

Today, as a result of sexual acceptance, teenage female sexuality is only considered pathological when it is associated with other behavioral problems such as depression and a florid infantile fantasy life amongst teenagers, we have seen a rise in sexually related crimes.

EMPLOYMENT OPPORTUNITIES

The opportunities of employment for females have increased the woman's availability to commit crime. These opportunities have caused white collar crime and corporate offenses to dramatically rise. Whereas years ago, the percentage of white collar offenses where primarily committed by men.

The women who make it up the managerial ladder to high-status positions rarely commit these offenses. There have been instances where the high positioned women commits embezzlement and fraud, but the majority of these offenses are committed by less prestigious and lower status positioned women.

Females are thought to be the weaker sex, a world wide stereotypical view, but statistics prove otherwise. For example, in 1988 there were an estimated 3.2 million arrests of women and although they only account for 22% of all arrests, these numbers are very high when you look at all statistics ever recorded.

A century ago, women made up approximately 1% of all crimes committed as opposed to the 99% of all crimes committed by men. Annually, women make up about 2.1 million of the violent offenders arrested. Based on self-reported victims of violence, women account for 14% of violent offenders.

To take it a step further, women accounted for about 16% of all felony convicted by years end in 1996.

8%	was for violent crimes
23%	were property-related crimes
17%	were illegal drug charges

The following statistic may not sound very impressive when trying to demonstrate the severity of females and crime, but I can assure you that a serious problem is at hand.

In 1988, about 1% of the female population within the United States was under the supervision of the correctional department.

1% of the female population accounts for 950,000 women either in prison, county jail (either awaiting trial, or serving time), on close supervision outside in the form of parole or probation.

In 1996, women made up 10% of the county jail population nationwide and that percentage was unchanged for 7 years prior, since 1989.

A sad and disturbing fact is that almost half of the women ever to be jailed, 48% were reported to have been either sexually or physically abused prior to being incarcerated and 27% were reported to have been raped.

In state prison, women made up approximately 6.6% in 2001. This was up from 1995 when women made up 6%.

CHAPTER FIVE
PEER/GANG PRESSURE

IN THIS CHAPTER, I would like to review the impact that peers and gangs have on the influence in criminal behavior. Of course, everyone growing up is the subject to the pressures from their peers. Just how influential are peers, depends on the individual's ability to withstand the pressures.

Almost everyone has a breaking point in which they conform with other individuals and allow their influence to disrupt their better judgement. It's the extent of their conformity that can lead to deviant behavior.

To demonstrate just how influential peer pressure can be, I'll tell about my first criminal experience and how my "best friend", at the time, encouraged me to assist in an auto theft.

When I was about 12½ years old, I had ran away from home and was without shelter. I went to a friend's house and spent the night. The next evening, we wanted to go to another friend's house that was located in another borough, far from where we were. My friend informed me about a car that was accessible to use as a means of transportation. Due to the fact that we didn't have any funds to travel, he suggested that we "borrow" the car. Although I knew right from wrong and the legal repercussions if we were caught, I didn't want to offend my friend and decline to participate. I also didn't want to seem scared in the face of a challenge. So we "borrowed" the car and drove it around until we were apprehended and charged with auto theft.

I had a second choice that night, but I chose to ignore it and allow peer pressure to overcome my better judgement.

Did my first criminal experience lead the way to a life of crime? In all honesty to my myself and my readers, I can tell you that it may have played a significant role in introducing me into a life of crime, but it was not the main cause.

Unfortunately, many people that have participated in a crime or used an illegal substance did so with the encouragement from his peers. This influence can cause a snowball effect increasing the risks of criminal behavior.

For the first half of this century, juvenile gangs were often the context where young men and women learn the values, skills, and motivation necessary to begin a criminal career. In fact, to this day, we can see how much influence the participation in a gang has over its members. If the majority of a gangs members decide to commit a crime then all of the members must participate, or will be subject to punishment.

Gangs have caused individuals that knew the difference between right and wrong to participate in illegal activities. Whereas, if the individual had never become a member, his chances of being involved in committing a crime at the time would be dramatically reduced.

The desire for a person to join a gang is more complex than societies assumptions. There are many factors as to who joins a gang and why. Ordinarily, geographical areas play an important part with the increase in membership in gangs, but with the increase of the teenage revolution and independence we've seen a dramatic change in where gangs are becoming increasingly popular. Now teens in suburban areas have increased their membership and criminal activities. Years ago, a gang outside of an urban area was more of a friendly gathering with very minor criminal activity and some drug use.

The factors include, but are not limited to:

- ★ Protection
- ★ Peer Pressure

* Family Environment
* Gangs as Families
* Acceptance

Each individual that joins a gang has his own motives for their membership. It could be one factor or a combination of several.

PROTECTION

Often times, an environment is so dangerous and riddled with crime that many young people decide to join a gang simply as a means of protection. Or they have already endured physical or mental abuse and don't wish to be a victim anymore.

Revenge can also play a part because an individual is tired of being a victim and decides to join not only as a means of protection but as a means to get back at his tormentors.

PEER PRESSURE

As stated above, peer pressure is a very important factor in a person's decision to join a gang. His/her friend may be a member of a local gang and the desire to join to be with that friend is very encouraging.

FAMILY ENVIRONMENT

There are many current gang members that grew up in a family environment where family members are involved within a gang. The child growing up assumes that being in a gang is acceptable. This distorts the child's views and increases the child in possibly becoming a member.

One of the most common causes for this occurrence is when an older brother or sister involved in a gang, especially one that the child looks up to. They try to copy their older siblings behavior as a means to bond with them.

GANGS AS FAMILIES

Many members join gangs because the gang treats them as family, a type of bonding that they lack from other sources. This is how many gangs are formed and will continue to grow in their increase in membership. Let's face it, most people need that emotional bonding and attention from someone and gangs provide that missing void.

ACCEPTANCE

The desire to feel and be accepted is very important in the attraction to become a member. The mere mention of a feared gang is enough to fuel an individual's desire to join. The individual may feel that joining the gang will give him the acceptance of his community by either fear of the gang or the gang's notoriety in that area.

Whatever the reasons that causes an individual to join a gang, in order to understand why that person joined, you would have to examine that person's history and current situation before questioning why he joined. It would be inappropriate and naive to come to a conclusion as to the reasons into that persons involvement.

Criminal behavior, like behavior in general is learned in interaction with others, mostly in intimate groups. To learn criminal behavior consists of acquiring both the criminal techniques, the motives, drives, and the attitudes associated with criminal behavior.

A person becomes a criminal because of an excess of definitions favorable to violation of the law over definitions unfavorable to violations of the law. Therefore, someone is relatively likely to become a criminal if the person's values and the values of the individuals who have the greatest influence over him more strongly favor criminal behavior.

Until now, the main topic of this chapter was the psychological reasons why someone would join a gang and the influence gangs have on involving criminal activities. Let us now review on who becomes gang members and the statistics with gangs as a whole.

The word *gang* simply means a group of persons involved in antisocial or criminal behavior.

As of 2002, the nationwide count of reported gang members have surpassed 600,000. When you think about it, that's a lot of people participating in antisocial and criminal behavior and the count for membership enrollment continues to climb especially now, due to the increase in today's gangs as opposed to the gangs years ago. This increase in membership enrollment can be attributed to not just peer and social pressures, but also the monetary gains gang participation encourages.

80% of all gang members that were asked whether they ever sold drugs before, while in a gang, admitted that they had either as a whole (the entire gang involved in the sales), or individually.

Since close to 43% of all gang memberships include a membership payment, it's easy to see why members choose criminal activities as a way to pay for gang dues and daily expenses.

Then when you account for the age of joining members, which is 12 to 13, well they obviously can't obtain a legitimate job especially one that pays well so their next obvious choice is to commit crime.

Many gangs are very organized and have a chain of command that begins with the leader, all the way down to the recruits. Many gangs chain of command vary from gang to gang so there are many different chains and the leader or president always have the control of every event that concerns basically every aspect of the gang.

Although, more than half of gangs today have written rules that every member must adhere to (66% to be exact) every gang follows so type of rules that all it's members must follow. Usually, gangs write and rewrite these rules over time and as the gangs expand geographically, the rules may be altered to correspond with that area's acceptance and ability to follow the rules.

Over 50% of all groups nationwide participate in a weekly meeting to discipline any members that break a rule, initiate any new members in the gang, analyze strategies on turf, gang structure, or financial situation. These meetings can either be participated by all members, or just the chain of command.

Society assumes that almost every gang is segregated in race or color, but the reality is that approximately (72%) of all gangs consist of members from a variety of ethnic backgrounds.

Although, a little less than half of all gang members are African Americans (48%), it's still assumed that Hispanics are leading in gang participation, but their numbers are somewhat lower with (43%). Asian gangs attribute to only (5%) of gang membership. While Whites only attribute to (4%). These numbers alter year to year, but as of the publication of this book, these are the current statistical numbers in gangs nationwide.

Since many members know that the rest of society frowns on gang activity and participation it's easy to see why so many members avoid telling their relatives as well as people around the community as much as 33%, that's one third, concerning their gang enrollment. What's to be ashamed of if they believe in the gang's cause? So, that leads to the next set of statistics.

Of all the gang members within this country, more than half have tried to quit the gang they were in and 80% wish they never participated in the first place. These numbers are staggering when you think about how gang awareness programs could prevent many people, especially teens, from joining a gang in the first place. A prevention program could lower the crime rate as well as reduce antisocial behavior from becoming a problem.

CHAPTER SIX
CRIMINAL PATTERNS

WHEN YOU HEAR about a career criminal or habitual offender causing havoc in some part of this country, you may wonder what exactly are those titles mean. Of course, if you think about the titles, they become self-explanatory.

* A career criminal is someone that chose crime for an occupation.
* A habitual offender is someone that continuously commits crime in possibly no order.

Although, the two definitions are, for-the-most-part, related and basically the same; there are many more definitions.

The word criminal pattern is loosely defined as: "A sample of a person's criminal behavioral, acts, or any other reliable features that characterizes any individual's behavioral, personality, or mannerisms."

Another word often associated with pattern and crime is Modus Operandi (MO). The term Modus Operandi basically means the same thing as criminal pattern, but it's somewhat more precise when examining crime and pattern.

The Federal Bureau of Investigation (FBI), has a department that is specifically aimed at targeting the MO's of serial offenders of specific crimes. Their job is to develop a profile on offenders based on the crimes, the locations of the crimes, any physical evidence recovered at the scene, any eye witnesses accounts on the crimes, the profiler's theories, and crimes in the past that may be similar in anyway. They use this data to compile a profile on the offender.

Over the years, the FBI has compiled data from apprehended serial criminals to get a better understanding on:

1. Why did they commit their crimes?
2. What motivated them?
3. How did they commit the acts?
4. How did they elude capture?
5. In what way can the FBI prevent a crime, similar to theirs from happening?
6. What was the offenders background like?

More often than not, serial criminals are eager to help the FBI with their profiling studies. Their underlying reasons for assisting could vary from individual to individual, but the majority that assist are either trying to relive the crime as they're being interviewed, or like the fact that their interviews may become public. Their reasons vary, but the majority of serial offenders don't assist simply because they are trying to help. There will always be an underlying reason.

Profiling is a science and for the most part has helped in the capture in many cases that have graced the department's desk. A science yes, but not without flaws. The FBI has been known to be wrong in many cases, like the DC sniper case.

It was assumed, due to the FBI's criminal profiling department that the shooter was a middle aged white male, driving a white box truck, that was anti-social (a loner) and probably lived with his parents; but nothing was further from the truth. Actually, almost every single detail in the profile was incorrect. The DC sniper was two black males, living out of their dark colored car, not a white box truck. So as you can see profiling isn't an exact science, it's an educated guess at best.

The only way to distinguish one criminal pattern from the next is to, not only investigate the criminal's illegal actions, but also, if possible, the crimes that the offender didn't get caught for.

Often times, the Criminal Justice System just examines the current offense and the offender's past criminal record. Without understanding why the offender committed the crime in the first place, or why did the offender even begin committing crime? How will they assist in the person's rehabilitation process if they don't do their homework into why the crimes were committed in the first place.

Looking at the Justice System from the respected, never been in trouble citizen's point of view, it's easy to be disillusioned into thinking that the wheels of justice are running smooth, but it's unfortunate to inform you that this is not necessarily the case.

Grant it, rehabilitation is the main objective and has to come from within, deep within the incarcerateds mind, body, and soul. It's up to the inmate to decide if he wishes to continue on the path of destructiveness or decides that he has had enough of the illegal activities and wishes to become a productive member of society. But what many inmates need is a push in the right direction. Most inmates has the ability to stagnate and finish their time without doing anything constructive.

Drawing upon my own experiences with the United States Justice System, I can tell you that my own rehabilitation has been an extensive battle, fighting my conscious all the way. I can now say, in all honesty and pride that I've finally taken an in-depth review of my entire life and realized that I needed to change. Not only the way I thought, but also my attitude. As I've said before, change has to start from within and it was up to me to want to make this change.

Fortunately, I saw what other people saw in me all this time, a generally smart individual that has made the wrong choices in life. That's the key word, "choices", for without them I wouldn't have had the choice to change.

Unfortunately though, I've committed a number of offenses over the years and regret every single one of them. But I can't change the past, only work on the future. But I will, forever be judged by not who I've become but who I was. Is this fair? Yes and no.

In order for someone to become rehabilitated, they must examine their actions from both perspectives, his/her current state of mind, the victim, and how the inmate can use the Department of Corrections to assist in their healing.

The Department of Corrections is for the most part, structured to punish convicted felons and hope that the inmate has learned from their incarceration not to commit any more crimes. What they should do to determine an inmate's true rehabilitated status is to obtain an in-depth report from the officers and staff that are around the inmate on a daily basis. They are the people that could inform the Department of Corrections whether or not the inmate is truly rehabilitated.

Before I continue, I'd like to explain what rehabilitation is. This way it will give the reader a better understanding and comprehension as to how an inmate must change.

REHABILITATION

To restore to a condition of good health, the ability to work, etc.

The concept is understood, but it's definition lacks true meaning when referring to inmates.

When a person decides that he/she is emotionally and physically tired of the vicious cycle of living a life of crime, only then will he begin the rehabilitation process. The cycle of committing a crime, getting arrested, serving time, only do it all over again is extremely tiring.

There are many reasons for a person to come to terms with reality and realize that committing crimes as a means to support their life style. Their problem isn't societies desire to keep them in their immediate environment or prevent them from paying next months rent. There's a deeper underlying problem that's within the person's own insecurities. Many people lack trust in the government as well as their own society and would rather struggle and commit crimes, instead of searching for a job.

Below are several excuses criminals use to justify their illegal activities as opposed to living within the laws of their society.

- ★ Many feel that they are incapable of obtaining employment due their criminal record, or are too insecure of their work abilities.
- ★ The fear of rejection may cause reluctance in even attempting to seek employment. Many may give up on job hunting after the first couple of denials.

- Many feel that upon obtaining employment, they will fail at their responsibilities and get fired from that job.

FIRST TIMERS

When a person decides to commit a crime for the first time, whether he/she is eight or eighty, they set their destiny in motion for the possibility of leading a life of crime.

Of course, crimes of opportunity fits into this category, no doubt about it, but first timers, more often than not, leads to a second time and possibly a third.

Upon interviewing a group of over fifty inmates, criminologists concluded that an individual who committed a crime at an early age, was more likely to commit crimes as they grew. This is attributed to the individual's assumption, in that persons mind, that since he got away with the first crime, they can get away with another one. This wouldn't occur if the person received therapy early on, he would be more susceptible to lead a crime free life.

A person, older in age, that commits a crime for the first time is less likely to continue his behavior. They realize that crime comes with penalties and they outweigh the rewards.

What I mean by first timers is someone who commits a crime, whether serious of not, with the intentions of committing that specific crime. I'm not referring to the kid that steals a piece of fruit from the corner store; although that is considered a crime. I'm referring to the type of crime that requires the assistance of the authorities.

Often times, murders occur as a first time offense. If the individual is ever released, they often go on to lead productive lives.

- One of the most important factors that prevent people from obtaining legal employment is the salary. Many feel that they should be making a lot more money, even if they are not qualified, in a legal job, so they feel that an illegal job would give them the appropriate pay they deserve.

The reasons behind a person's choice to begin a life of crime vary. It depends on the individuals reasoning that initiates his/her criminal activities. If we were to put the criminal's actions into logical reasoning, we would know, logically, that there are no justifiable reasons for anyone to commit crimes. But in the criminals mind, his actions are justifiable. Especially if his immediate environment condones his behavior and he is surrounded around criminal behavior.

Why do some people have difficulty remaining law-abiding citizens while the majority of the world's population behaves in accordance with their countries laws? Whether the reasons include an economic melt down or the person's own insecurities prevent him from obtaining employment, the fact remains the same, crime is crime and there is no justification for committing one.

There are five basic criminal types that we need to examine to grasp a greater understanding as to how and why crime is committed. I'll start from crimes of opportunity, to first timers, to criminals with short term goals, to the habitual offenders, and finally crimes of passion.

CRIMES OF OPPORTUNITY

These crimes often occur in job related situations. Often times the normally law abiding citizen, sees the perfect opportunity to commit a theft and acts upon it. This form of white collar crimes often happens due to an opportunity that presents itself within their job. This form of crime is called Embezzlement. It's when an employer commits a theft within his/her own company. A large percent of these type of crimes go unreported because of lack of evidence.

Most people that steal from big companies fail to realize that their theft from a big company is still a theft. They try to justify it with a variety of excuses. But no matter what excuse they use, their actions are still considered illegal.

Another form of opportunity theft is when someone comes across an opportunity to steal property that doesn't belong to them. This type of crime happens so often, especially ones that go unreported, that the statistics cannot give an accurate number.

When I was approximately 11 years old, I was riding my bike around the neighborhood when I came across several moving men hauling furniture into a van. My curiosity got the better of me as to who was moving out, so I stayed and watched.

Down the block, I noticed a group of four teenagers walking up towards my direction. Upon reaching the moving van, one of the teens noticed that the van was unoccupied because all of the moving men were in the apartment building retrieving more furniture. This teen saw an opportunity to grab a box from the van and run. He didn't even care what was in the box, he just swiped it.

The other three teens saw that their friend got away with the theft and they followed suit. It was that simple. The opportunity presented itself and an individual, with larceny in their heart, took advantage of a situation to commit a crime.

Prisons are filled with stories of how an opportunity to commit a crime presented itself and someone took advantage of the situation. After all, it's not very hard to realize just how easy it is to observe throughout the day how many opportunities are present to commit a theft by chance. It's up to the individual to know the difference that a theft is still considered illegal no matter if it was planned or not.

SHORT-TERM GOALS

In the numerous conversations and interviews I've had over the years in prison, I've discovered that as odd and strange as this may sound, many criminals have created their own form of retirement plan. Criminals often set goals on the length of time they plan to commit crime and how much money they plan to save. As a result, most of the drug dealers I've interviewed, said that upon release they'd continue to sell drugs for a six-month period and then "retire" with whatever profit they acquire from their illegal sales. While others state that once they save a certain amount of money, no matter the time period, they will "retire".

Another form of "retirement" they plan for is saving enough money to purchase a business and live off the profits from their own legal business with hopes of maintaining a legal lifestyle.

There have been instances where criminals do incorporate their ill-gotten gains with legal businesses, but they are exceptions. The majority of drug dealers are often disillusioned by the grand life. They see fictional drug dealers in movies, or hear about the king pins that ruled entire metropolitans and assume that they can achieve instant riches with ease.

Unfortunately, their illusion of grandeur causes them to receive a nice stiff sentence in the prison system and a criminal record. The percentage of drug dealers that actually achieve kingpin status is very low, almost as low as a basketball player turning pro.

Whatever the crime, a criminal with a goal is very dangerous because no matter what, he/she will continue to commit crimes until his goal or arrest. For the criminals that do reach their intended goal, they more than likely don't terminate their life of crime. Their assumption is that since they've reached their intended goal without any serious difficulty, they can continue their life of crime. Actually, this way of rationalizing their continued illegal actions are due to several factors.

One is evident, their greed for extremely quick wealth has increased their living habits and has caused a never ending cycle of crime to support their lifestyle to which they've grown accustomed to. With the advancement of their living status comes the need to fund it with more money. This form of living is often their downfall because even if the authorities can't arrest you for your criminal actions they can investigate how you've acquired the money you live off with no apparent legal job. Your salary wouldn't amount up to your lifestyle because if it did you wouldn't need to commit crimes in the first place; Although, it's been done by people. Just look at Al Capone's situation. The federal government couldn't arrest him for any direct crime so they arrested him for tax evasion.

The second reason why they can't stop committing crimes is psychological. The intense emotional rush a person feels committing a crime causes the person to continue committing crimes to feed that psychological rush. It's a sort of obsessive, similar to the euphoric feeling that an illegal drug causes.

With certain environments, being a part in criminal activity is a way of life and a form of status within itself. This is most often the case in poverty stricken areas, usually in big cities.

As I've stated before, a criminal with a goal is a danger to himself/herself and their community. It's unfortunate that this continued behavior is constant and that leads to the next topic, habitual offenders.

HABITUAL OFFENDER

Although the general definition is self explanatory as to what a *habitual offender* is. It's somewhat more complicated than that.

Habitual is, of course, an act being repeated over and over without an apparent end. But, when we use this word incorporated with the law, the definitions become somewhat blurred and distorted. For the sake of the reader, I'll define *habitual* in understandable terms so I won't confuse the reader.

The three strikes law, that I'm sure you've heard about on television and in newspapers refer to a twice convicted criminal that was given a life term for a third conviction. This is usually given to someone that was convicted of the same type of crime three times. The courts feel that there's no chance of rehabilitation after the third time so it's best for society to sentence him to life imprisonment. Whether this form of punishment is right, is not appropriate to argue at this time. I'm merely stating facts. I'll leave it up to my readers to draw their own conclusions.

One type of *habitual offender* is a person that continuously commits the same crime over and over again. Although, many criminals have multiple convictions for the same offense, they usually reserve the three strikes law for violent offenders. California is the only state known that can give a man life for stealing a slice of pizza. Other states have adapted the three strikes law, but labeling it differently. One state may refer to it as the career criminal law and another as a predicate law. Whatever they call it, it still results in the same outcome, *life in prison*.

Another type of *habitual offender* is when a criminal is convicted of three crimes regardless of the offense. States with this guideline for habitual offender status tend to be much stricter and give out sentences with higher numbers in years.

Many habitual offenders are drug addicts that tend to continue in the never-ending circle of drug use to crime to prison, and repeat the cycle all over again. I personally know that drugs have a grip over the user and may cause the user to commit multiple crimes. I'm not condoning any addict's violation of the law simply to obtain anything of value to purchase drugs. If he/she weren't on drugs no violation of law would be broken. I'm simply saying that we need to aggressively address the problem of addiction to stop this cycle from occurring time and time again. Prisons are filled with addicts with no will nor desire to change their habits. This unfortunate habit of committing crime, multiple crimes to support ones addiction will either result in death from a drug overdose, or a sentence under the habitual offender act.

Being a habitual offender doesn't mean that you are incapable of changing your criminal habits. That is farther from the truth. Humans are creatures of habit. So, once a habitual offender realizes that his negative actions always result in negative consequences, he can change his habits that result in positive outcomes. But, until the offender *realizes* (the key word), that committing crime hasn't produced desirable results only then will he change.

CRIMES OF PASSION

It would be easy to write that crimes of passion happens as a result of jealousy and revenge, but it's somewhat more complicated.

True, most crimes of passion resulted from jealous and/or revenge motives, but then you have the political motive that has turned countries upside down.

Everyday, someone either murders someone or attempts to cause extreme physical harm to someone else because of his or her jealous emotions. Everyday, you'll hear about someone's attempt to kill a loved one in a rage. And, how often do you hear of a celebrity arrested in crimes related to revenge and jealousy.

The psychological control jealousy has over an individual is immense. Everyone has experienced bouts of jealousy throughout their lives of different degrees. It's up to each and every one of us to determine whether or not the importance of our emotional state is worth getting into trouble. But, many people allow emotion to cloud their otherwise rational judgement. Ordinarily, a rational person would analyze a situation and determine its importance and then find a solution. But, a jealous man/woman has tunnel vision and only wants one outcome to the situation, revenge.

Politically, emotional crimes occur very often. Many times leading to assassinations and government coups. In this country, political crimes of passions occur often. The assassination of John and Robert Kennedy was a crime of passion. Was there any governmental conspiracy or not? We'll never know, but the main reason for their deaths was a passionate emotion. Someone believed that their death would fulfill his/her emotional state. Whether it was political, revenge, or someone that didn't like the way they were running the country.

The majority of people assume that crime is just crime and that all criminals are the same but that is furthest from the truth as you have read.

Assumptions about crime that we hear and see through all media cloud our judgement and cause us to assume that a bank robber is the same as a purse-snatcher. I hope the reader can now view each crime as a separate action as opposed to believing that a crime is just a crime.

Emotions high in demonstration.

Prisoners of war in Afghanistan.

Attitudes change with transference.

Typical court house.

Social environment.

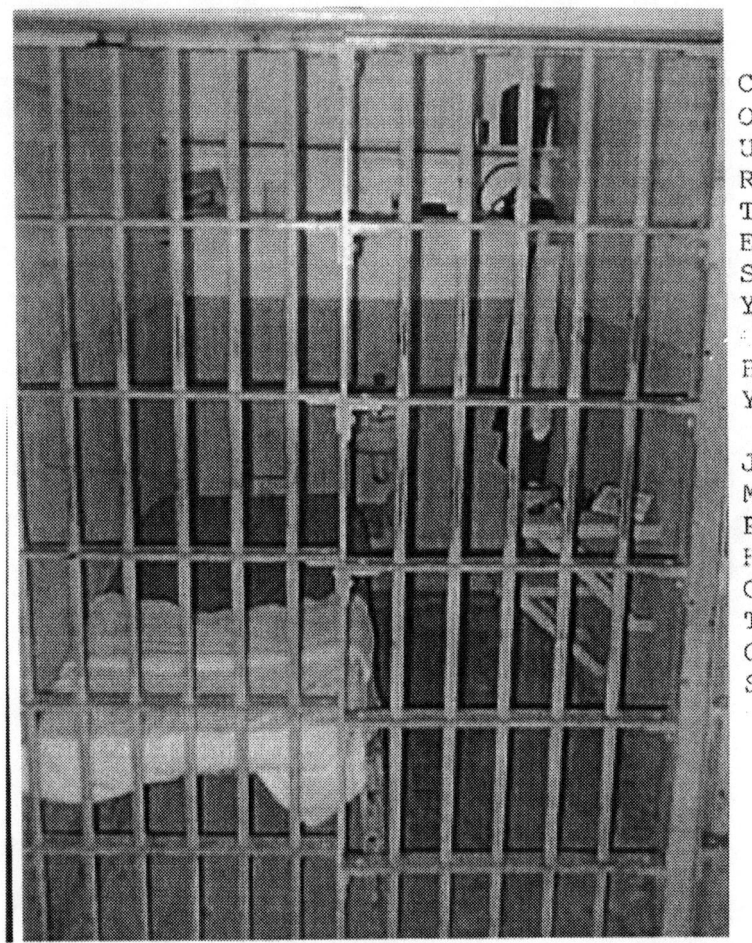

Typical prison cell.

PART 3
CRIMINOLOGY 303

CHAPTER SEVEN
CRIME

WHEN WE HEAR about a crime that happened, most Americans become transfixed and yearn to learn every detail. This phenomenon happened because of the increase in crime and then the media's need to report it. There used to be a time when only major crime was reported; now every crime seems to be reported. This has desensitized most Americans into accepting crime as a way of life. Especially now, certain local and cable stations specifically target court battles and criminally related programs. Our acceptance possibly increases the crime rate because many criminals get ideas from shows on how to commit a crime.

Not long ago, the concept of an entire state relocating the residents, being constructed into one huge prison, doesn't seem so far fetched. Especially now, with the increase prison construction on the rise.

Many people with a limited amount of knowledge in law, would assume that crime is just crime. This is not the case. A crime may have similar characteristics of other crimes, but each and every crime should be handled in the same manner. But each case is different. Special attention to specific crimes should be addressed, like a serial rapist should receive therapy targeting that crime. Or the drug dealer, he should receive treatment to awaken the individual that there are other avenues to obtain money, other than committing crime.

In this chapter, I will give the reader a brief overview of the most recognizable crimes. This will give the reader a better understanding on each crime. There are thousands of laws in each state and it would be impossible to write them all. And besides, each state differs in the sentencing guidelines and definitions of each crime.

Many states have laws that may be impossible to impose in another state. For instance, states with volcanoes have numerous laws pertaining to volcanoes. So their laws are incapable of being enforced in other states.

Every crime, within the legal guidelines of each state, should be mentioned in this chapter, but that would take us away from the main topic of this book. And, it would become a study guide for criminal law instead of criminal behavior. I broke down the legal definitions of each crime so the reader, for those of you that don't know, can understand what crime is.

Of course, breaking the law is one of the main topics in this book, but it's not the main subject. The importance is the criminal's mind set to commit these acts, not just the acts themselves.

There are exceptions in the courts views of a crime. Take for instance, when a person injures or even kills someone out of protecting themselves or a loved one. The District Attorney may deem that your method of protection was questionable or that you may have used too much excessive force. Many laws state that if a person feels that he or she is in danger, they should contact the authorities and wait for them to handle it.

Many states though, have the self defense law enacted. Stating that if the use of force was inevitable to prevent injury or death then the act is justified. But beware, if a situation can be avoided by police intervention, then by all means do so. You wouldn't want nor need the hassle.

In order to find out the laws pertaining to self defense in your state, simply contact a lawyer, the local police department, the Department of Law and Public Safety in your state capital, the Prosecutors office, or go to your local library.

MURDER

Violent crimes are perhaps the most feared type of crime there is. Many Americans greatly fear the prospect of getting murdered. Most murders happen after social interaction between the victim and the person that committed the act. The social interactions between the two parties often have a strong impact as to the outcome of the crime. Many emotions are involved.

In a substantial amount of cases, the victim often initiates the violence perhaps by the attempts to cause physical harm towards the other party. Furthermore, most people who kill lack any psychotic tendencies.

What's more, is that studies indicate that men have a higher tendency to cause the death of someone by their hands than women do. Women studies also indicate that men kill, or are killed eight to ten times more than women and the reasons are different with gender.

Women are more susceptible to murder because of a deep rooted emotion that was caused by the victim, or simply trying to survive a brutal attack, or greed. Their reasons are often clearer as to their actions as opposed to the reasons behind men who murder.

Other studies show that the summer seems to have more homicides than any other season. Whether the heat is the cause for such increased violence is a possibility, but still isn't an argument in a court of law.

The act of taking a life is the ultimate criminal act. When you cause the death of someone, there is no way a victim can overcome all the emotions involved with being a victim of a crime.

What compels an individual to kill another human by force, or other means depends on a variety of factors. The reasons depend on the motive for the death because for every murder that occurs there's a reason for the act to have been committed.

MURDER

The actor purposely causes the death or serious bodily injury resulting in the death of the victim.

This occurs when the actor, acting alone or with one or more persons, is engaged in the commission of, or an attempt to commit or flight after committing or attempting to commit robbery, sexual assault, arson, burglary, kidnapping, car jacking, criminal escape, or terrorism and in the course of such crime or immediate flight there from, any person causes the death of a person other than one of the participants.

CASE FILE

A Toms River insurance agent began an extramarital affair with Sarann Druashaar, a married woman, in June 1983. As early as December 1983, defendant mentioned to Kraushaar the idea of killing his wife, Maria. In May 1984, defendant met Robert Cumber of Louisiana and questioned him about hiring an "investigator." Defendant later telephoned Cumber, who referred defendant to Billy Wayne McKinnon, a former sheriff's officer from Louisiana. Defendant agreed to pay McKinnon $5,000 to meet him in Atlantic City on June 18, 1984, and offered to pay him $65,000 to kill his wife. In addition to the $5,000 that McKinnon had already received, defendant agreed to pay him $10,000 up front and $50,000 from the expected insurance proceeds on his wife's life. At that meeting defendant paid McKinnon $7,000 and gave him a picture of his wife. Defendant told McKinnon to kill her that evening, when defendant would be present. In preparation for the killing, defendant and McKinnon discussed various ways to kill Maria. Defendant believed that he would not be considered a suspect because he was considered an outstanding citizen with influence in the community.

McKinnon did not carry out the murder at that time, but instead returned to Louisiana. Defendant communicated with him on numerous occasions and sent him additional money. Under pressure from defendant to complete the job, McKinnon returned to Atlantic City on June 19, 1984, and met with defendant, who proposed a second plan for the killing to take place that evening. Defendant told McKinnon that he would leave his wife in their car to be executed while defendant went into a restaurant under the pretense of using the bathroom facilities. However, McKinnon did not commit the murder at that time either. Defendant, persistent in his effort to have his wife killed, offered McKinnon an "extra fifteen" ($15,000) if he would return to New Jersey a third time to do the "job" before Labor Day. McKinnon agreed, and, on September 6, 1984 he and defendant met at a service area parking lot located south of Toms River. Together they selected a spot on the Garden State Parkway to carry out Maria's murder and made final plans for the slaying, which was to occur that evening. The plan was to make the murder look like a robbery.

September 6, 1984, under the pretext of an evening of dining and gambling, he met McKinnon outside Harrah's at approximately 9:30 p.m. and told him that he and Maria would be leaving the casino at about midnight. Defendant also asked McKinnon for the return of the photographs of Maria and of their home that he had given him in June. As previously arranged with McKinnon, defendant pulled into the Oyster Creek picnic area at milepost seventy-one on the Garden State Parkway at about 12:30 a.m. on September 7. While his wife lay sleeping on the front seat, defendant got out of the car under the ruse of needing to repair a flat fire. Defendant squatted down to prepare himself for being hit on the head as part of the simulated robbery. Maria Marshall was shot in the back twice. She died immediately.

When the police arrived on the scene, defendant continued to make the murder look like a robbery. The State argues that defendant showed no remorse after the crime, but pretended to join his three sons in grieving over the loss of their mother.

The State argued at the trial level that he even staged a suicide attempt. Defendant protested his innocence then and continues to do so now in explanation of his conduct. Defendant's claims of innocence soon unraveled. Telephone records traced him to McKinnon, who turned State's evidence. In exchange for a plea to conspiracy to commit murder, McKinnon implicated Marshall and identified a Louisiana man, Larry Thompson, as the triggerman.

Investigation disclosed that during his planning, defendant had been increasing the insurance policies on his wife's life. At the time of her death, Maria Marshall's life was insured for about $1,400,000. Defendant had been paying his wife's premiums while neglecting his own. Defendant hastened to complete an application for a policy for a home mortgage before the murder. On the last day of her life, Maria underwent a physical examination for that policy. The State offered proof that defendant could have been motivated to kill by rising debts incurred in his business, including a $128,000 home-equity loan and a short-term bank debt in excess of $40,000. While amassing those large insurance policies, defendant also continued his relationship with Sarann Kraushaar, with whom he had intended to live after the murder.

A jury acquitted Thompson of the murder but accepted McKinnon's version of defendant's role and found him guilty of conspiracy to commit his wife's murder and of murder-by-hire. The only aggravating factor submitted to and found by the jury was that defendant had hired another to commit murder. The two mitigating factors submitted to and found by the jury were that defendant had no history of criminal activity, and the catch-all mitigating factor. At the time of the offense defendant was forty-four years of age, and had been involved in charitable and community activities. The jury unanimously found beyond a reasonable doubt that the aggravating factor outweighed the mitigating factors. The trial court sentenced defendants to death.

MANSLAUGHTER

Criminal homicide constitutes aggravated manslaughter when:
The actor recklessly causes death under circumstances manifesting extreme indifference to human life; or

The actor causes the death of another person while fleeing or attempting to elude a law enforcement officer; or

A homicide, which would otherwise be murder, is committed in the heart of passion, or emotional state that would otherwise constitute murder, but fall under manslaughter guidelines.

VEHICULAR MANSLAUGHTER

It is estimated, by the department of transportation, that an estimated 10,000 to 20,000 people die of vehicular homicide each year.

Alcohol related vehicle deaths are the most common among the causes and the unfortunate fact is that young people make up 65% of the total.

Another way to cause the death is behind the wheel of a motor vehicle is to accidentally crash do to negligent behavior, which can also mean that you ran a red light, or were driving in an erratic behavior that killed a pedestrian on a sidewalk or killed a passenger in your vehicle.

If the death can be legitimately proven to be an accident and nothing more, then you won't be charged with any crime.

Unfortunately, even though most people know the dangers that driving under the influence, or driving in a behavior that can illegal, like speeding, people continue to do it with little regard as to a possible deadly outcome and that's why the authorities have begun to seriously crack down and punish offenders severally for their actions.

The actor causes the death of another person by negligently operating a motor vehicle or vessel recklessly.

If the actor was operating the motor vehicle or vessel while under the influence of any intoxicating liquor, narcotic, hallucinogenic, or habit forming drug; or

If the actor was operating the motor vehicle or vessel while his driver's license or reciprocity privileges was suspended or revoked at the time of the crime.

ROBBERY

The most common motive behind a robbery is of course greed. The violator wants what the victim has of value and is willing to forcibly take it. In urban areas, especially in New York City, the unwritten rule to really experiencing what the city is about, or to become a "true" New Yorker is to get robbed. It has come to actually become a sort of rite of passage to be a victim, an acceptance that being robbed is a way of life.

Robbery, in legal terms are very precise as its definition. It states "Robbery is a crime of second degree, except that it is a crime of first degree if in the course of committing the theft the actor attempts to kill anyone, or purposely inflicts bodily injury, or is armed with, or uses, or threatens the immediate use of a deadly weapon."

This does not exclude the use of any object that although is not an actual working weapon it is assumed by the victim that it can cause physical harm if the actor chooses to use it and in the event if the victim does not comply with the actor.

CAR JACKING

Until the early 1990's "car jacking" as we know it today was unheard of by the general public. In Newark, New Jersey, an epidemic of car jackings caused a national outcry when it began to spread to other states.

Prior to creating this law, the penalties for such a crime were relatively small. Now with this new law, specifically for this crime the penalties are severe.

The law stipulates that a person is guilty of car jacking if in the course of committing an unlawful taking of a motor vehicle if the actor inflicts bodily injury or uses force upon an occupant or person in possession or control of a motor vehicle.

SEXUAL OFFENSES

Ten years ago, there were approximately 240,000 people convicted of a sexual offence charge. Today those numbers have increased somewhat. Additionally, about 25% of those convicted of a sexual offense charge had been on a community release program, either probation or parole. This is probably due to the lack of programs structured at sexual offenders.

The availability of "date rape" drugs, (drugs that are odorless and colorless and renders the victim unconscious when the actor is able to have someone ingest it), increased the numbers dramatically. These drugs include, but are not limited to, Rofenals and Ketamine. Their street names are roofies and special K.

What's odd in a violent offender's mind is that they generally don't consider themselves as criminals. They often consider themselves as "different". This particular mind set, often increases the offender to repeat the offense.

Usually, the offender and victim live in the same geographical area. The act is usually within a short distance of the offenders home. Also, about half of the rapes that occurred, the offender and the victim knew each other prior to the crime. But, this type of rape isn't reported because the victim usually believes that the violation was their fault and they feel guilty.

Additionally, rape victims often don't report the crime because of shame, feelings of guilt, disgust, and humiliation. What also causes the victim reluctant to notify the authorities is the fear of their spouse or mate leaving them because of the violation. This does occur, because the mate may become overwhelmed by their spouse's violation.

Many offenders use this knowledge to their advantage. This is another reason that there is no exact data as to how many rapes occur in the United States.

The legal definitions are as follows:

Sexual Penetration:
Means vaginal intercourse, cunnilingus, fellatio, or anal intercourse between persons or insertion of the hand, finger, or object into the anus or vagina either by the actor or upon the actor's instruction. The depth of insertion shall not be relevant as to the commission of the crime.

Sexual Contact:
Means an intentional touching by the victim or actor, either directly or through clothing, of the victim's or actor's intimate parts for the purpose of degrading or humiliating the victim or sexually arousing or sexually gratifying the actor. Sexual contact of the actor with himself must be in view of the victim whom the actor knows to be present.

DRUG CHARGE

A C.D.S. (control of a deadly substance) is the possession of an illegal drug. Whether you wish to consume the substance or try to sell it is of no consequence to this charge because its very precise about its wording. The person in question is in control of a substance that can be considered dangerous.

An illegal drug is any drug that was not legally prescribed to them by a certified medical doctor or a substance that has no medical usage for that individual or is considered dangerous to anyone that consumes it.

There are many drugs that are manufactured in an illegal form for the sole purpose of illegal consumption and without any legal medical benefits. These drugs are the most severe and carry the most punishment.

DRUGS

The legal definitions are as follows:

Administer:
Means the direct application of a controlled dangerous substance or controlled substance analogy, whether by injection, inhalation, ingestion, or any other means.

Controlled Dangerous Substance:
Means a drug, substance, or immediate precursor and any drug or substance, which when ingested, is metabolized or otherwise becomes a controlled substance in the human body.

In chapter eight, you will find a list of numerous drugs and their effects.

ASSAULT

The legal definitions are as follows:

Simple Assault:
The actor attempts to cause or purposely knowingly or recklessly causes bodily injury to another; or

Negligently causes bodily injury to another with a deadly weapon; or

Attempts by physical menace to put another in fear of imminent serious bodily injury.

A simple assault is a disorderly person's offense unless committed in a fight or scuffle entered into by mutual consent, in which case it is a petty disorderly person's offense.

Aggravated Assault:

The actor attempts to cause serious bodily injury to another, or causes such injury purposely or knowingly or under circumstances manifesting extreme indifference to the value of human life recklessly causes such injury: or

Knowingly under circumstances manifesting extreme indifference to the value of human life points a firearm in the direction of another whether or not the actor believes it to be loaded.

KIDNAPPING

The legal definitions are as follows:

Kidnapping:

Holding for ransom, reward, or as a hostage. A person is guilty of kidnapping if he unlawfully removes another from the place where he is found or if he unlawfully confines another with the purpose of holding that person for ransom or reward or as a shield or hostage.

Holding for other purposes a person is guilty of kidnapping if he unlawfully removes another from his place of business or residence, or a substantial distance from the vicinity from where he is found, or if he unlawfully confines another for a substantial period, with any of the following purposes;

To facilitate commission of any crime or flight thereafter. To inflict bodily injury on or to terrorize the victim or another; to interfere with the performance of any government or function, to permanently deprive a parent, guardian, or lawful custodial of custody of the victim.

PROSTITUTION

It has been said that prostitution is one of the oldest professions ever. Now whether that statement is true or not is a matter of opinion and I am in no position to dispute that fact.

Prostitution is the act of receiving money or gifts of value for a sexual favor. Any sexual act at all from full fledged intercourse to the client watching the prostitute perform some sort of sexual act for mere pleasure.

The misconception that many people have is that prostitution is a woman or man walking the streets searching for someone to have a sexual relation with for monetary gain, but it's more complex than that. The N.T.F.P. (The National Task Force on Prostitution) has concluded that only about 20% of the prostitutes work within the United States. It is estimated that about a million women have prostituted themselves now or in the past.

The typical street prostitute is the most dangerous form of prostitution. That is due to the fact that the prospective client could be cruising for a client simply to inflict bodily harm. That's why the majority of prostitutes work through other means to attract clients. Some may seek clients via Internet or place ads in newspapers and magazines, but a large majority of prostitutes tend to work in a safer environment like a massage parlor or through an escort service. I won't include the brothels in Nevada because they are legal establishments that are permitted to allow sexual favors for money.

CHAPTER EIGHT
ILLEGAL SUBSTANCES

DRUGS

T HE POPULARITY BETWEEN crime and drugs practically coexist as one. With so many crimes related to drugs today, it's easy to determine that drugs fuel crime and increase the population of institutions. What I mean by institutions isn't limited to just prisons. Others include:

> Jails
> Drug Rehabilitation Centers
> Halfway Houses
> Mental Health Facilities
> Residential Drug Treatment Centers
> Narcotic and Alcoholic Anonymous Centers
> Adolescent Drug Placement Facility

One of the problems with the majority of these institutions is that they don't concentrate on the victims that were caused by their drug addictions. Victims aren't just limited to a stranger's encounter with a drug-addicted individual. They also include:

The Drug Addict's Relatives
The Addict's Friends
The Addict's Co-workers
Their surrounding society
The Victim's Relatives
Etc.

When a person begins a drug habit he/she not only hurts themselves, but they also effect everyone associated with that addict's problem. With the increase of the habit, comes a need to fund that habit. That's when crime, serious crime, comes into the picture then the victim ratio begins to rise.

Although the mere possession of an illegal drug and being under the influence is a crime, it is when the addict takes his addiction a step further and begins committing criminal offenses that really need to be addressed as an issue. For without the drug, there would have been no crime.

The victim associated with a drug addict's criminal offense should receive counseling to reduce any emotional scarring and to show the victim the cause for the crime. Many victims of criminal offenses never learn the reason why the criminal committed the offense in the first place. This counseling wouldn't be to justify the crime, it would assist in understanding why the criminal committed the offense.

If the majority of drug users were to be cured and maintain their sobriety, prisons would become dramatically depopulated. If you take into consideration the entire drug related crimes that result in incarceration you would see how populated prisons are due to this epidemic.

Let's examine drug-related crime that plague our society and prisons from the most severe to the least severe.

THE BREAK DOWN

I'm now going to break down, in order, how drugs travel from one person's hand to another until it reaches your hands. The average person doesn't realize how many people are involved in order to make those drugs easily obtainable.

At the very top of the drug chain are the growers. They are the ones that cultivate numerous plants associated in the manufacturing of illegal drugs. Of course, not all drugs are manufactured from a plant. Underground chemists create a whole variety of illegal and often deadly drugs.

Once the crop is ready to be harvested, they negotiate with manufacturers for the best price. (Manufacturers are the ones that create illegal drugs from raw materials). These manufacturers hire chemists to make the drug ready to sell. These manufacturers, upon completion of their product, sell in bulk to distributors from around the world. Whether these distributors have a large operation varies.

The distributor then negotiates a price with local street dealers and drug king pins. King pins usually have a huge operation in one area, either in a town or even an entire state. Whereas street dealers concentrate selling their illegal wares in their own neighborhood or other neighborhoods in close proximity to their own.

Both street dealers and king pins have a local clientele and feel more comfortable in dealing with the same people to reduce their chances of arrest and/or the victims of a robbery.

Depending on the quality of the product will determine their success. Which leads us to the drug user. He/she may commit various crimes to support their habits. To get technical, the purchase of an illegal drug is a crime in it self.

Imagine if we were to take into consideration statistically, the amount of arrests associated with drugs annually, the numbers would be staggering. The amount of money spent on collecting data would be enough to exceed the deficit of most third world countries.

If I were to inform you that most inhabitants of this earth are addicted with one form of drug of another, you would probably balk at the very idea. I didn't say just illegal drugs, mind you. Many mind altering substances are so integrated into our everyday lives that society doesn't refer to them as drugs. Why you ask, well what respected citizen wants to consider themselves as drug dependent.

Let's examine the three most common drugs, legal drugs mind you, that are integrated in our daily lives and used in so many products that you may of never of known.

Caffeine

Caffeine is a bitter tasting alkaloid that is usually found in many beverage products such as coffee, (one of the most widely used caffeine products available). Many teas, sodas, and juices have caffeine in their products. Many medications and some foods have trace amounts of caffeine in them also. This drug is one of the most widely used products known to man and it is a very powerful stimulant.

Nicotine

Nicotine is a highly toxic liquid alkaloid found in all tobacco products. This chemical works in many mind altering ways. It often works as a stimulant as well as a reliever for many stress related emotions.

The bad part is the serious health risks associated with its consumption. Due to the amount of law suits now filed against big tobacco companies, either by relatives of family members that died because of the tobacco product or the government trying to get their piece of the pie, it was the surge in law suits that caused the price of cigarettes to skyrocket. So much so that the price has increased several hundred percent over the last couple of years. Of course, if the government didn't enforce the tobacco companies to place strict warning labels on their products about the serious health risks associated with smoking, the companies would have continued to keep the public in the dark.

Alcohol

One sad statistic related to alcohol is that the majority of drinkers have no inclination about the production of alcohol and the serious side effects on the body.

When someone becomes intoxicated from an alcoholic beverage, the chemicals go directly to the brain and acts as a depressant. It begins to strip away inhibitions and can cause the person to become very reckless in judgement. This is the leading cause for most of the DWI accidents.

Alcohol is a colorless, volatile, and flammable liquid produced by the fermentation of carbohydrates or a synthetically made chemical compound similar to carbohydrates.

It's evident that these common ingredients increase a persons health risk, as well as their mental health, with continued use. If you realized how much negative effect it had on your body, you would reduce, if not quit that product immediately. The said chemicals eat away healthy cells and contaminate and pollute the body with toxins. Every mind-altering drug creates their effects by changing the activity of the brain by hindering or accelerating the transmissions of messages at the brains numerous switching points, perhaps by also changing the increase and decrease in the brains chemical elements.

Other substances that are used for illegal purposes have medical benefits. The most lethal drug in existence, heroin, helps patients with serious pain. Morphine is manufactured from the same plant that makes heroin. Even prescription drugs, like sleeping pills and other medications can be abused to "get high".

Now let's examine the most "popular" illegal substances and the chief physio and psychological effects they have on the body when consumed.

Then we'll see what an overdose of that drug can cause when taken in excessive amounts and abused.

And lastly, I'll explain what a person subcomes to when they are going through a withdrawal from the lack of said drug. The withdrawal effects alone should be warning enough to deter the reader from ever considering ingesting any illegal drug.

CANNABIS

When inhaled or ingested, you feel euphoria, your inhibitions are relaxed. Users tend to over indulge themselves on food, especially junk foods. Although the physio effects are similar to the effects of an overdose,

I'm going to list them because they relate to the current state the person experiences at the time of indulgence. They include, but are not limited to, an increase in the heart and pulse rate, dizziness, anxiety, and feelings or paranoia.

THE EFFECTS OF AN OVERDOSE:

Although the effects from cannabis cannot cause death, they may make you feel like death is a possibility. The symptoms include:

    Anxiety
    Slowed reaction and movements
    Paranoid
    Distorted sense of time
    Loss of concentration
    Hallucinations

THE EFFECTS OF WITHDRAWAL:

Trouble sleeping, (insomnia) and hyperactivity are two common systems associated with withdrawals. The person going though withdrawal may experience other symptoms that are created in the persons mind. Fortunately for the daily user, if he is unable to obtain any, he won't have any lasting effects.

NARCOTICS

This is determined to be the most dangerous drug in the world. Its illegal use claims the lives of many of its abuser. The effects cause the user to feel euphoria, drowsiness, slowed breathing, excessive itching, and most often times extreme nausea.

THE EFFECTS OF AN OVERDOSE:

    Slowed and severe shallow breathing
    Very clammy skin

Convulsions
The user could slip into a coma
Loss of concentration

THE EFFECTS OF WITHDRAWAL:

Most users that withdraw from either heroin or morphine tend to develop flu like symptoms, watery eyes, a runny nose, loss of appetite, irritability (everything bothers them), panic attacks, tremors, extreme headaches, the chills, sweating, stomach cramps, nausea, insomnia, and either constipation or diarrhea.

STIMULANTS

Stimulants are often confused with hallucinogens, but they are not in the same family of drugs. A stimulant is either cocaine or an amphetamine based pill.

Now-a-days, with the advancements in illegal drug production, a stimulant can also be found in new designer club drugs such as ecstasy or speed. But these new designer drugs are often times a collective of several other chemical compounds and are therefore unclassifiable with the conventional list of illegal drugs.

THE EFFECTS OF AN OVERDOSE:

When taken, a stimulant effects the physio and psychological body with the below symptoms.

Hyperactivity
Feelings of euphoria
An increase in pulse and heart rate
An increase in blood pressure
Irritability
Severe bouts of insomnia that can last for weeks
Loss of appetite
Aimless behavior

Often times, a person is too delusional to realize that anymore consumption may cause the users death. Agitation and an increase in body temperature are common as well as panic, convulsions, hallucinations, and body racking tremors.

THE EFFECTS OF WITHDRAWAL:

The user going through a withdrawal from a stimulant based drug may become irritable, have long spells of sleep or no sleep at all, depression, and apathy.

DEPRESSANTS

Depressants are often in prescription drugs that is prescribed by a physician. When taken inappropriately, the drug becomes dangerous.

What causes the following the effects is abuse of the drug. The abuser views becomes distorted, drowsy, speech is slurred, and often exhibits behavior that could be mistaken as those associated with alcohol.

THE EFFECTS OF AN OVERDOSE:

When an excessive amount of the drug is ingested, the user begins to have the following symptoms:

>   Shallow breathing
>   Cold and clammy skin
>   A weak or increased pulse rate
>   The possibility of slipping into a coma
>   A weak or increased pulse rate
>   And death

THE EFFECTS OF WITHDRAWAL:

When the user can't get another prescription from their doctor or they decide to quit, they may suffer from bouts of insomnia, become anxious, have tremors, go through delirium, have convulsions, and could possibly die as a result from lack of the drug.

HALLUCINOGENS

There are more types of hallucinogens that exist on this green earth than most people realize. Most are extracted from their natural form and consumed as is. To give the reader of how natural and to what lengths people will go through to extract their drugs from this earth, read on.

Imagine yourself in a cow pasture on a warm summer night. You are impatiently waiting for dawn to break so you can begin your search for the mysterious magic mushrooms. But these aren't any ordinary mushrooms, these are special mushrooms that when consumed will take you on a journey to a world of visual and audio distortion co-exist with reality.

Now that you can visualize this semi-pleasant scenario, envision yourself searching the cow and horse pastures for manure, yes manure, at the dead of night. See these hallucinogenic mushrooms grow in fresh manure and only survive at night. Once the sun rays hit it they die.

Now in order for you to extract this precious drug, you are going to have to stick your hand into the feces to pull the fungus from the feces. You may be there for a while though, when you begin to extract it you don't want it to break apart. So you'll have to be very delicate in separating the manure. Once you extract the precious drug you can either consume it right there or bring them home to wash off the feces. Then you can make a tea out of it.

What some people go through to get high.

Oh, one more thing, I neglected to tell you. There is another type of mushroom that grows in the same way, but this one is deadly. The only way to tell them apart is to look under the cap. The one that has dots underneath the cap and the other one doesn't.

Now that I made you realize that not all drugs are natures way of saying that drug use is permitted, let's look at the effects hallucinogenic drugs have on the physio and psychological body when consumed.

When a person consumes this type of drug, hallucinations will occur, just how severe depends on the type of drug, the body weight of the user, and the quantity taken. Paranoid behavior, distorted body and surrounding images and anxiety will happen. The physio effects are tremors, bouts of nausea, chills, an increase of pulse and heart rate. And quite possibly, amnesia. Fortunately, it is very rare for a user to take daily. The user would have to ingest a double or triple amount to "get high" on a daily basis.

THE EFFECTS OF AN OVERDOSE:

> Either a temporary or permanent contact with reality
> The user can have a seizure
> The user can fall into a coma

I've had friends slip into an illusional world. Sometimes they stay in this fictional world and have to be hospitalized.

THE EFFECTS OF WITHDRAWAL:

Fortunately, hallucinogenic drugs have no withdrawal effects when the user cannot obtain the drug. This makes the transition easier.

INHALANTS

These drugs are extremely dangerous and can cause long term effects but the enticement to use them is the availability and legal possession. The user can find these types of drugs in a wide assortment of glues (hydrocarbons), that can be bought in any hardware store.

Then there are the airesol sprays that users often inhale, these are called whippets, (nitrous oxide).

When inhaled in any form, the user feels euphoria, giddiness, excitement, loss of inhibitions, aggressive behavior, bouts of delusions, headaches, depression, nausea, and drowsiness.

THE EFFECTS OF AN OVERDOSE:

The cronic user often succumbs to the following symptoms:

Confusion
Weak memory
Unstable balance
Erratic pulse
Increase heart rate
Possibly death

THE EFFECTS OF WITHDRAWAL:

When the user goes through withdrawal stages, he/she will often experience insomnia, loss of appetite, often suffers from depression, irritability, and extreme headaches.

With all of the side effect symptoms a user endures while under the influence of the drug and the stages of withdrawal, you would think that the user would quit.

But . . .

With the popularity of drugs and the temporary "high" people get from using them, illegal drug use will be available until governments find a way to stop cultivation of the drugs and the creation of chemical compounds for inhalant products.

When prescribed and not abused, many of the drugs listed above do have medical and therapeutic benefits. It's when a person takes it inappropriately that the drug not longer has medical benefits. On the contrary, the drug can become lethal.

Individuals vary in response to each drug. How quickly a person becomes addicted depends on many factors. For instance, how available is the drug, how often and in what quantity it is abused, and the users physical condition and psychological makeup.

After the user experiments with drugs, some users believe that they are unable to cope with life without them. Their continued use of the same drug creates a vicious cycle. As the user relies on the drug to feel in control, he/she repeatedly confirm their belief that they are powerless to cope without it.

With their deterioration to function without the drug becomes more powerful, it becomes strengthened by the increasing dependency. That dependency becomes a full-blown addiction. The chemical dependency strengthens the notion that the user can't cope with life without the drug.

Until the addict realizes that his real problem is the substance and nothing more, then and only then will he be able to quit. But until then, his life will continue to increase with problems.

DRUG STATISTICS

Drug charges account for a huge portion of incarcerations nation wide. It's been estimated that on any given moment, there is someone being arrested for a charge related to drug. (please review this chapter to see how many ways there are to be arrested in connection with drugs).

By years end of 2000, 57% of all federal inmates were incarcerated for a drug offense. This percentage was higher than the previous year. A large percent of those numbers can be attributed to smugglers from other countries trying to bring contraband into the United States.

In the same year, there was an estimated 21% of all state inmates incarcerated for drug offenses.

One extremely disturbing fact is that between the years of 1990 to 2000, drug offenders that were incarcerated in Federal prisons accounted for 59% of the population.

Alcohol is perhaps the worst offender in crimes associated with drug use. Due to the fact that mere possession, consumption (in moderation), and manufacturing are basically legal within the United States, many citizens abuse alcohol beyond the limitations of the law.

Court houses are clogged with alcohol related cases everyday. This is because the assumption is that since alcohol is legal, it's acceptable to drink beyond the recommended consumption.

One crime in particular that is related to alcohol is drunken disorderly. In a ten year period, the increase has risen 44%. This crime refers to exhibiting drunken behavior in a public area, other than a bar or any other establishment that sells liquor.

The biggest offense related to alcohol drunkenness is (DWI) driving while intoxicated. On any given year, there are approximately 10,000 alcohol related deaths from driving. Drivers assume that they are not impaired enough from drinking to drive.

Other crimes related to alcohol consumption fills the legal system in astronomical numbers. Below are some statistics about alcohol related convictions.

In 1996, there were approximately 5.3 million people that were under the supervision of a correction agency. Out that total, two million were to have been under the influence of alcohol during the offense. That's about 36%. But the vast majority, about 1.3 million were convicted and sentenced to community supervision.

Out of the 1.5 million offenders, 1.3 million were sentenced to community probation and approximately 200,000 were on parole.

Among the violent offenders that were under the influence during the commission of the offense:

>41% were in a county jail
>Of that, 41% were sentenced to probation
>38% to a state prison
>21% to a federal prison

These numbers will continue to climb if we don't educate the youth about the dangers of drinking alcohol. This way, they will be aware of the hidden dangers associated with drinking.

CHAPTER NINE
PRISON INVOLVEMENT

PRISONS IN THE USA

WHEN YOU HEAR the word prison mentioned on the news, the mind becomes flooded with images of cell bars securing violent criminals that are ready to attack you at a minutes notice. But in all honesty, prison is a society unlike any other on earth. The stereotypical assumptions about prisons are semi-correct and at best vague in the intimate details. Prison is a society unlike any environment in existence. The survival techniques alone would amaze you and the complexity of how the prison society is run is unbelievable.

With the United States prison population expanding to nearly two million by 2005. Looking at the numbers, it's easy to realize the importance of rehabilitation. Additionally, it's been estimated that by the year 2004, one in fifteen American citizens will of done time or will be incarcerated in their life time. With these statistics, it's important to understand why there is a need for a more aggressive approach to the rehabilitation process. Prevention methods on deviant behavior is needed to stop this vicious cycle from continuing.

What's more interesting is the fact that approximately 65% of all people in America have been incarcerated due to a crime related to drugs. This drug epidemic doesn't cease at the halls of Justice once someone is convicted of the crime.

Prisons are heavily contaminated with drugs. Every illegal drug imaginable can be found within prison walls. That is as long as the prisoners funds enable him/her to purchase them. That's because drugs in jail are very expensive.

What's sad is the fact that I've personally witnessed fellow prisoners enter prison with no illegal drug habits only to become addicted to something while incarcerated. Then that prisoner is released onto his society with a drug habit that will more than likely be financed through crime. Now that person's chance for a new life is destroyed. Granted, it was his decision to use drugs in the first place but if a rehabilitation system, that worked, was in place to give that inmate other possibilities, then that inmate would have a fighting chance.

It's unfortunate that while incarcerated, this new addict has no one to turn to if he desires to quit. If this person realizes that his new destructive habit will ultimately be his downfall and tries to seek help from staff, he will fear expressing his need for assistance for fear of an institutional disciplinary charge. This strain is very hard on the addict because he is incapable of seeking appropriate help. Then there are the continuous flow of drugs around him with his fellow inmates encouraging him to continue his use. It's not like being free where if someone desires to quit using drugs he can move to a different town to reduce the temptation.

Aside from drugs, being incarcerated causes all of your fears and self-criticisms to build inside of you. This can either break him down emotionally or make him more resistant to his inner insecurities.

In my first book, "The Official Guide to Interrogation", I dedicated an entire chapter to imprisonment and confinement. I would like to share several important passages to emphasize the effects that confinement has on the prisoner.

CONFINEMENT

Just the mere isolation in a confined state, void of a lot of human contact, will expose the subject to psychological states that can break any resistant barrier and encourage full compliance.

Results of confinement are simply a series of events that occurs deep within the subjects mind and progress as confinement extends.

The psychological breakdown is as fellows.

1.) The deprivation of sensory stimuli induces stress.
2.) The stress becomes unbearable and penetrating for most subjects.
3.) The subject has a growing need for physical and social stimuli.
4.) Some subjects progressively loss touch with reality, focus inwardly, and produce delusions, hallucinations, and other psychological deteriorating effects.

Having first hand experience in confinement and isolation deprivation has enabled me to understand the psychological penetration of how the mind operates in confined areas. It's unfortunate that many inmates can't handle the pressures of being confined. I've witnessed grown men break under these pressures and fall into deep depressive states. Many that suffer from depression either have no understanding as to the cause of their depression and refuse to seek professional assistance. This is because pride and the assumption that only "crazy" people meet with members from the psychology department.

Confinement is usually restricted to a very small cell. Generally, a prison cell is approximately 5' by 9', give or take a foot. Each cell is equipped with a metal toilet/sink combination, a one inch thick mattress as a bed, a small ventilation that really pushes accumulated air from within the prison into your cell, and a locker to put all of your property. And above all, dirt and dust that has been accumulating since the construction of the prison. Very few inmates clean their cells from top to bottom and those that do seem to be placed in the worst conditioned cells.

The mere strain of isolation from the outside world can cause the inmate to put all of his concentrations into doing his time.

Prison cells tend to be very stress inducing and have been known to cause many inmates to psychologically break down. Stir crazy is the common phrase for it.

Prisons structured for reduced custody inmates usually house inmates to dormitory type settings. Similar to army barracks. This form of confinement induces a different type of emotional stress. Dormitories prevents the inmate from having any privacy. Forcing the inmate to share every waking minute with anywhere from 12 to 120 inmates.

GANGS

In this day and age, the prison population is filling up with violent gangs. A prisoner can either remain neutral, which means that he will not join any gang, group, or organization during his incarceration. Or the inmate will seek the companionship of a gang. In that instance, the gang becomes that inmate's new immediate family. His new family will fill the void for companionship and friendship.

Within the last several years though, prison administrations have cracked down on prison organizations, even going so far as creating entire units for members of gangs. These units have strict programs targeted at breaking up the groups and forcing them to disavow their memberships. If the member does not comply with the program within the unit then he will stay there until he does. These units are harsh and they tend to force the inmate to disavow their membership to the administration, even if they don't mean it.

These units have caused a reduction in membership but groups will continue to exist, especially targeting to the lonely and/or scared. There will never be a prison to be gang free.

All inmates, neutral or not, have to follow the rules and regulations created by the population and every inmate tends to adhere by them. They are the unwritten laws within the inner prison society that every prisoner must follow. Most of the rules aren't illegal in a sense, but some are frowned upon by the administration. But, often times there are conflicts with the rules created by the prison society and the rules of the administration. Many times an inmate becomes caught between them and feels immense pressures from both sides. These pressures can induce great stress if the inmate doesn't know which side to choose from. To go against the administrations rules can result in institutional discipline, that could result in the inmate to do more time. But to go against the rules of the prison can ostracize him and possibly cause a violent reaction to occur.

LACK OF INSIGHT

Over the years of my incarceration, I've come across many prisoners that refuse to take responsibility for the actions that caused their incarceration. Many view their actions as just and honestly believe that their actions were forced upon them because society forced them to commit crimes. They assume that society is oppressing them from obtaining a good job and not allowing them from getting out of their current community. This oppression is assumed to be because of either their race or their culture. Of course that is not the case in 99% of all incarcerations.

Granted, there are a few exceptions were the inmate really hadn't committed the crime. But they are far and few between. Far below the cries of injustice heard everyday within the walls of every prison across the nation.

LEARNING

Unbeknownst to the outside world, for many inmates, prison is a learning environment enabling inmates a chance to learn new and better techniques on how to commit a variety of crimes.

In every prison or institution in the world, an inmate has the ability to learn how to commit every crime imaginable. There will always be inmates eager to share their criminal experiences and criminal knowledge. This is a form of boosting their ego and gives the inmate the ability to boast about how he committed various crimes and gotten away with them. It's amazing how much energy and brain power a criminal applies to create illegal acts.

Idle time allows inmates the ability to formulate new plans once that prisoner is free. That's why I'm an advocate for reform programs that target key areas. Without them, your money will continue to warehouse people that would otherwise be good for rehabilitation.

FAMILY

Being isolated from the free society and loved ones often does more harm than good. With the only ability to interact with loved ones is through the telephone, mail, or a visit once a week for one and half hours, it restricts the inmate to fully grasp the family structure. This sometimes causes a severe strain on relationships. Many inmates lack the insight as to what to do in daily family situations or crisis. Problems arise within the family structure, like in a marriage, problems with finances, opening a simple bank account is new to them.

Some inmates will never develop and maintain a healthy relationship with the opposite sex. This is due to the fact that they never visualized that form of bonding within their own household while growing up.

With so many obstacles inmates face it's not hard to assume what route they'll take if times get rough in the free society.

RELIGION

Many inmates turn towards religion as a spiritual outlet. Prayer helps many inmates through their time. But unfortunately, it's rare that they take their belief to the streets upon release.

Below I had listed four reasons why inmates turn to religion while incarcerated.

1.) Often times, inmates were raised in a religious household and religion is the first thing that an inmate will seek out for comfort.

2.) Guilt plays an important role in new conversions into religions. There are many inmates that seek religion to ease the burden of a guilty conscious for the crimes they had committed.
3.) Some prisoners believe that becoming religious will assist them with the parole board, thinking that the board will assume that the prisoner is rehabilitated. But they are mistaken, parole boards concentrate very little on a prisoners spiritual awakening.
4.) Many times inmates turn to religion as a means for protection. Because practitioners in that religion will not allow anything to happen to one of their religious brothers.

Religions are so strong in prisons that the mere disrespect can cause a riot or severe protest to erupt at a moments notice. It's common knowledge that religion is one of the worst emotionally charged subjects a prisoner can discuss.

ATTITUDE

In prison, the overall attitude that causes the most problems are pride and respect. The combination is the number one factor for prison violence. Detention units are filled with inmates that received detention time for an infraction by lack of regard for the rules within the prison. Some of these units are harsh and extremely punishing to the inmate. Of course prisons don't want to be lenient with offenders. But they should take the inmates mental and physical health into consideration with inmates in detention units.

The need to be respected fuels emotions to run high and causes the inmate to carry this emotions with him upon release. It becomes a natural reaction to act in a defensive manner. Any assumed disrespect can cause an assaultive crime from being committed if the recently released inmate feels disrespected.

Incarcerations often causes bitterness and resentment within the prisoner. They were never taught how to properly release their frustrations, so they lash out often times committing crimes as a release, thinking that lashing out in a defensive manner is the only way for release from frustrations.

TALENT

Prisons are overflowing with an extremely large amount of talented people. If those inmates only knew how to channel their gifts and use it in a productive and constructive manner, prisons would be reduced in populations. Many inmates just use these talents to make a little extra money and/or pass the time. It's unfortunate that their talent could assist in rehabilitation. Additionally, they fail to realize the potential they possess.

I've witnessed artists and craft makers that have the ability to make anything they put their minds to with a minimal amount materials. Their talents are worthy of known art galleries. They either don't have the confidence in themselves or just lack the insight to their true abilities.

There are also inmates in prison that study law, with barely a G.E.D., fighting their legal arguments worthy of many prestigious law firms. They have become so dedicated and drawn to the laws of justice that they know the letter and the spirit of the law better than some lawyers. Their para-legal skills would secure their future indefinitely. And then there are those that are dedicated to helping others and win motions that their own lawyers couldn't have achieved.

The amount of writers and poets incarcerated are astounding: I'm a prime example. I was fortunate to discover that I had talents. And as you can see, I now use my gift to inform the world with my thoughts and experiences. If only the rest of the writers could gain the confidence and patience to write what they wish. Many people have come to me expressing their desire to write about their life story or that of a loved one. But most are either too lazy or lack the confidence enough to put pen to pad.

Others may not have enough education to write with confidence. This discourages them more by embarrassment. I often try to encourage them into taking up school to increase their vocabulary and grammar.

Hopefully, my words of wisdom encouraged them enough to fulfill their life long dreams.

The poets in prison have the talent worthy of popular greeting cards, but are content with letting their talents go to waste. I've read poems that moved me so deeply that they inspired me to write to try and capture a poem close to the emotional impact that so inspired me.

With all of the talents hidden behind the walls of America's prisons, you would assume that the recidivism rate would be dramatically lower. I say this because the inmates time would force him to realize that his gift can create a new life for him upon release. Sadly, most inmates need a boost of encouragement and a little guidance to tap their raw talents into becoming careers on the other side of the prisons walls.

For some time now, I've been considering instructing a writers workshop for the authors and poets within my facility to sculpture their raw talents. I believe that teaching a course like that would help people gain the confidence they need to stop their cycle of recidivism. Also, the course may even help with my rehabilitation. I've learned that in life, help can be found in the strangest of places. They might enlighten me to a different style of writing my books.

Unfortunately though, most inmates with a talent maintain a criminal mentality and continue to dwell on illegal activities.

Many inmates go through a series of phases while in prison. I, for one, have gone through many transitions during my incarceration. My rebellious behavior had placed me into detention for several long years. But I believe that my time in detention had forced me to face my actions head on. This was a blessing. It was a shame that it took several years confined in a cell, 24/7, for me to realize that I have great potential in writing.

Many people though, become bitter and angry because of their lack of desire to change. It's easier to blame everyone else for their imprisonment but themselves. This ignorance causes them to misdirect their faults and helps them cope with their incarceration because they feel that their actions were just.

The increase of prison populations are on the rise annually and will continue this uphill trend unless better rehabilitation methods are implemented.

I could continue to go on about prison procedures for reform, or lack of, but the basis of this book is to examine all aspects of criminal behavior. Prison in itself is a form of punishment due to criminal behavior, it is not the initial cause. Although, prisons can be a breeding ground for criminal acts, it was not structured for that purpose.

There is an old saying in prison that rings true and is fitting to end this chapter.

"You do the time, don't let the time do you."

What that means is that the inmate should do his prison sentence to the best of his ability and not let it get to him or the time will break him down.

STATISTICS ON PRISONS

To demonstrate to you just how prison construction is a booming business, I recently saw a documentary on the privatization of prisons. That means that private corporations, not necessarily associated with State or Federal backing, builds and administrates entire prisons for a profit. These prisons are run in accordance with state laws and designated to house prisoners. The only difference between a state run facility and a private one is the cost. A state run facility may charge the government $35,000 per inmate, whereas the private prison will charge the state less. The state in turn pockets the difference.

This market, of privatized prisons, has become so profitable that the corporations that run them, are now publicly traded in Wall Street as stocks. That means that with the money the corporation receives from investors, they can construct more prisons, which will increase their profits. More prisons means more money for the investors. In turn, investors will purchase more stocks.

In just seven years, from 1995 to 2002, the prison population grew an average of 3.6% annually. That means that every year the prison population increased 3.6% nation wide.

By years end of 2002, state and federal prison authorities estimate that they had under their jurisdiction, 1,440,655 inmates. 1,277,127 were under state jurisdiction and 163,528 were under the jurisdiction of the federal prison system.

Local jails held or supervised 737,912 persons awaiting trial or serving a sentence that same year. Another 72,400 of these were persons serving their sentence in the community.

The entire sum of people under the watchful eye of the authorities by years end of 2002, were 6.7 million people. That is not to say that they were all incarcerated, but what that means is that they were either in a county jail, prison, or on parole or probation. The census bureau calculated that 3.1% of all U.S. adult residents, or 1 out of 32 adults, in 2002, were included in the 6.7 million.

The 272,111 persons that were released in 1994, accounted for nearly 4,877,000 arrest charges over their recorded careers. These numbers are staggering when you think about it. That means not even a quarter or a million had committed nearly five million crimes.

The recidivism rate for persons that were released from prisons is a sad amount of numbers. The increase of recidivisms continue to rise every year with no end in sight.

For instance, in 1994, an estimated 67.5% of persons released from prison were either rearrested for a felony or serious misdemeanor within three years of their release. This find was discovered because 15 states that released 272,111 inmates tracked their return to prison.

By 2001, it was estimated that 2.7% of the entire adult population in this country, had served time in prison in some period in their lives. This percentage is up from 1.8% in 1991 and 1.3% in 1974.

Nearly two thirds of the 3.8 million increase in the number of adults ever incarcerated between 1974 and 2001 occurred as a result of an increase in the first incarceration rates; one third occurred as a result of an increase in the number of residents age 18 and older.

Another interesting fact is that nearly a third of former incarcerated prisoners, were still under the intense supervision of corrections upon release. These numbers include 731,000 on parole, some 166,000 in local county jails.

The population of prison inmates will continue to rise and rise. And with congress recently approving a practically unlimited budget for the Department of Corrections, it seems that there is no end in sight to a solution.

These statistics are depressing, even for a convicted criminal. It seems that going to jail is a sort of right of passage, now-a-days. It seems that only tragedies or horrific crimes bring about changes in the law. What about the tragedies of human lives associated with crime. No one win when a crime is committed. There are many victims, including you, the reader. Remember, if you're not part of the solution, you're part of the problem.

PART 4
CRIMINOLOGY 404

CHAPTER TEN
STATISTICS

SINCE THE UNITED States first began to track incarceration rates, approximately 5.7 million citizens had served a prison sentence in some point in their life time. This includes federal and state prisons. With almost two million of them currently the Department of Corrections. Statistically, increases in prison population are on the rise. And sadly, if the percentage of incarcerations remain the same, about 1 in 16 American citizens will of been convicted of a crime and sent to prison in some point in their life.

With the Justice Department estimating about 50 million crimes reported each year, it's easy to realize that crime is truly embedded in our society. They also estimate that the overall crime rate has increased somewhat in 2001, when the decrease in crime had fallen for the past 11 years. They aren't bad statistics considering that since 1991, the decrease in crime fell an estimated 26.4% by 2001.

ECONOMIC LOSS

Examine the chart below that the Federal Bureau of Investigation (FBI), made public in 1996. It breaks down the economic loss to the United States citizens due from criminal incidents.

CRIMINAL OFFENSES	$ LOSS	TOTAL AMOUNT OF $ LOSS
MURDER	$230	$4,130,000,000
ROBBERY	560	698,000,000
RAPE	236	40,000,000
ASSAULT	128	650,000,000
BURGLARY	840	3,999,000,000
PERSONAL THEFT	82	3,128,000,000
MOTOR VEHICLE CRIME	4,000	9,641,000,000
TOTAL		$22,286,000,000

CRIME IN NUMBERS

If we were to take into consideration the total cost of each crime, the loss to the victim and their family and the state would be extremely high. Let's break down the economic loss for a murder. The cost may reach into the millions.

First of all, if the murdered victim was the result of a robbery, the money loss begins with the crime itself. Then the state begins to lose money because they have to foot the bill for the investigation of the crime. The state would have to pay the salaries for the following;

       Police officers
       The forensic specialists
       Detectives
       Medical examiners
       The district attorney

And then if he is convicted of the crime, the Department of Corrections begins their bill for however long the convict has.

The victims family is stuck with burial costs and may be liable for any debt the victim accumulated prior to his death.

So as you can estimate from the above break down, a crime is very expensive. And with more than 50 million crimes reported each year, the price for crime is beyond calculation.

UNIFORM CRIME REPORT

Unknown to the majority of the public, except of course for those in law enforcement and legal occupations, has never heard of a program called The Uniform Crime Report.

This program began collecting data of crimes committed across the country in 1929, (the year of the great depression). They collected data from local law enforcement agencies.

Congress liked the idea so much that they enacted a law, title 28, section 534 of the United States code, that appointed the Attorney General to be responsible for the collection of all data related to crime. The Attorney General in turn handed down the responsibility to the F.B.I.

Below is a chart, dated 1996, on the most criminal offenses recorded since the UCR began collecting data. These numbers represent the crime rate out of 100,000 persons within the United States. Please take into consideration that they only represent crimes that were reported.

NUMBER OF REPORTED CRIMES

OFFENSE COMMITTED	NUMBER
MURDER	19,645
ROBBERY	537,000
RAPE	957,679
ASSAULT	1,029,814
ARSON	88,887
BURGLARY	2,501,524
LARCENY	7,894,620
MOTOR VEHICLE THEFT	1,395,192
DWI (DRIVING WHILE INTOXICATED)	1,467,300
ILLEGAL DRUG CHARGE	1,506,200

WEAPON POSSESSION	216,200
STOLEN PROPERTY	151,100
FRAUD	465,000
FORGERY / COUNTERFEIT	121,600
EMBEZZLEMENT	15,700
DOMESTIC VIOLENCE	149,800
PROSTITUTION	99,000
VANDALISM	320,900
SIMPLE ASSAULT / BATTERY	1,329,000
GAMBLING	21,000
LIQUOR VIOLATIONS	677,400
LOITERING / DWELLING	185,100
RUNAWAYS	195,700
PUBLIC DRUNKENESS	718,700
DISORDERLY CONDUCT	842,600
SEXUAL OFFENSES	95,800
VAGRANCY CHARGES	27,800
ÖALL OTHER VIOLATIONS	3,743,200
TOTAL	22,168,401

★ These violations do not include traffic.

MEN AND WOMEN

I would now like to show you some interesting statistics on the differences between men and women criminals and the differences in crimes they commit.

Of course, crime is a male dominated area and has always remained that way, and they will continue to stay well above in statistics for all major crime. The only exception is prostitution.

If you closely examine the chart below, from 1977, you will notice that males have a much higher percentage in arrest rates than women.

MALE AND FEMALE CRIME BREAK DOWN

OFFENSE	MALE %		FEMALE%	
	1977 – – – – 1996		1997 – – – – 1996	
MURDER	16.8	89.7	11.0	10.3
ROBBERY	15.4	90.3	25.5	9.7
ASSAULT	10.9	82.1	8.2	17.9
RAPE	65.0	98.8	38.5	1.2
BURGLARY	9.2	88.7	29.2	11.3
	N/A	66.2	N/A	33.8
THEFT	N/A	66.2	N/A	33.8
ARSON	8.9	85.1	5.1	14.9
MOTOR VEHICLE	N/A	86.4	N/A	13.6
ALL OTHER CRIMES	N/A	85.9	N/A	14.1

The above statistics, all calculate to a total of 100% for all crimes of that year. Whereas, the 1996 statistics are percentages that calculate for each crime.

The lifetime likelihood a person will go to prison is:

★ Men have an 11.3% chance
★ Whereas women have only a 1.8% chance
★ Blacks are the highest with 18.6%
★ Hispanic are second with 10%
★ Whites are last with 3.4%

As of 2002, it has been estimated that the percentages for first time incarcerations, during their entire lives are as follows:

★ Black males dominate with 32%
★ Hispanic males with 17%
★ White males with 5.9%

In 1997, the federal inmate population were more likely than state inmates to be:

★ Women (7% federal vs. 6% state)
★ Hispanic (27% vs. 17%)
★ age 45 or older (24% vs. 13%)
★ College educated inmates (18% vs. 11%)
★ Illegal immigrants (18% vs. 5%)

These statistics include state and federal institutions.

In 1996, out of 100% of all county jail inmates:

★ ¼ were held for a violent offense
★ ¼ were held for a property crime
★ one fifth were held for a drug offense

RACE

A very big topic within the criminal justice system are the differences between race and crime. There have been countless statistics and discussions about how race plays an important factor in crime statistics.

As recently as 2001, imprisonment was higher for:

Black males with 16.6%
Black females with 1.7%
Hispanic males with 7.7%
Hispanic females with 0.7%
White males with 2.6%
White females with 0.3%

These findings mean that out of the entire United States population, the above percentages are for per race, per gender.

Of about every ten inmates in the county jails, there are approximately 7 inmates that had previous convictions or were on probation.

Let's examine the statistical differences between county jail inmates versus prison.

In 1996, 63% of the jailed inmates were either racial or ethnic minorities, this is up 2% since 1989.

In state prisons nation wide, 64% of the prison population were of another race other than white. These findings were taken in 2001.

In 2001, out of 100% of all state prisoners:

★ 49% were incarcerated for a violent offense, (That's nearly half the population).
★ 20% were incarcerated for property crime
★ 21% were incarcerated for drug crimes.

HOMICIDE

Since homicide is the most violent crime known to man, let's examine the percentage difference of homicides committed by males and females from 1980 to 1997.

Males have increased homicide arrests, whereas females had declined somewhat.

NATION WIDE ARREST OF ALL HOMICIDES

MALE		FEMALE	
1980	1997	1980	1997
87.2%	90.6%	12.8%	9.4%

Many assume that the prison system is filled with adults older than 35, but this is farthest from the truth. The true figures are that only 24% of all jailed inmates were between 35 to 44 in age in 1996. There was a 7% increase from 1989.

In many state prisons, over half (57%) of the inmate population is under 35 by years end as of 2001.

The illegal immigrant population in all county jails were about 8% in 2001. Whereas, in prison, they only accounted for 4% of the total population. This is due to the fact that the majority of immigrants in county jails are there because of complications in their immigration status and not for a criminal offense.

By 2001, 54% of all county jail inmates had at least a high school diplomas or a GED. The state prison inmates percentage tended to be higher with 57%. This is due to inmates having the ability and time to enroll in school in the prison.

CONCLUSION

UPON THE COMPLETION OF this book, I hope the reader understands that in life, there is a lot more to criminal behavior than believed. And, criminal behavior doesn't just form in the persons mind without any assistance from his environment. Criminal intentions can be prevented if we restructure our societies way of thinking.

Until recently, I hadn't realized how much of an impact this book would have on me until its completion. It was then that I knew what my future held. I believe that I have an ability to help people in a positive way. Even if this book appealed to just one person and they decided to change their illegal habits, I'll feel like I've accomplished something.

Throughout this book, I spoke about how rehabilitative methods can decrease the statistics related to crime. But you'll also notice that I didn't give examples into what programs would be proper to construct in order to achieve this goal. That's because there is no one program that targets all forms of deviant behavior. Each area needs to be addressed. Some areas include, but are not limited to the following examples:

- ★ Drug Addiction
- ★ Crime Prevention
- ★ Environment Participation
- ★ Strong Family Structure
- ★ Increase Positive thinking
- ★ Decrease Negative Social gatherings

One of my downfalls and weaknesses can be attributed to idle time. As the old saying goes, "Idle time is the devils playground." That saying rings true on a personal level. At home, I had enrolled in a Tae Kwon Do class to keep me focused and physically in shape. The minute that I stopped going, I began to let negative behavior supersede my original positive objectives. I'm not justifying my illegal behavior to idle time, I'm merely showing the reader the effect idle time had on me.

Many people assume that just because I'm incarcerated that life ceases to exist. But my perseverance to strive to become better and someone of substance, encouraged me to become who I am today. I hope that this book helps at least one person on this earth to strive to become a part of the solution and not part of problem. I would know then that all of this writing wasn't in vain.

There is one person in particular that I would like to see affected by this book, and that's my beautiful daughter. I pray that until the day I am released, she doesn't head down the wrong path. It's up to her and no one else of the life she chooses to lead. Just like the rest of my readers.

I tried to be as honest and true as possible to everyone and I hope that you enjoyed my hard work. Set goals as I have and strive to be the best that you can, no matter where you are.

GLOSSARY

AGGRESSION — Expressing hostile behavior.

ANXIETY — A state of apprehension and uneasiness caused by fear.

APATHY — Absence of emotion.

ATTITUDE — Manner, feeling, or disposition with regard to a person, place, or thing.

BEHAVIOR — One's manner of acting or behaving.

BIOLOGICAL — Study of life in all its forms and process.

CENTRAL NERVOUS SYSTEM — The part of the nervous system comprising the brain and spinal cord.

COGNITIVE — The act or processing knowing.

CONFORMITY	The act of prevailing attitudes, social behavioral standards, etc.
CRIME	Any act that is considered illegal.
CRIMINOLOGIST	Someone that studies crime and criminals.
CULTURE	To live in accordance of social standards and continued from generation to generation.
CULTURE SHOCK	Bewilderment experienced from someone that is unaccustomed to a new culture.
DELIRIUM	Temporary disturbances a persons conscious state caused by delusion, excited states, etc.
DEVIANCY	The act of behaving out of the norm.
EMOTION	To feel strongly about something.
ENVIRONMENT	Immediate surroundings.
EPIDEMIC	Something that effects many people simultaneously.
EUPHORIA	A very strong feeling of happiness, well being, and emotional awareness.
GENES	A physical compound that is passed to the child from parents.

GENETICS	The department of biology that concentrates on heredity.
GENOCIDE	The intentional extermination of a race, nation, or political group.
HABITUAL	Pattern of actions as a result of frequent repetition.
HALLUCINATE	Experiencing illusions and delusions that do not exist.
HEREDITY	The passing of certain traits and characteristics from the parents to the child.
INCARCERATION	To imprison or institutionalize.
INFLUENCE	A power that persuades a person to change views, habits, attitudes, etc.
INHALANT	A substance that once inhaled produces a drug like feeling.
INSOMNIA	Incapable of falling asleep.
ISOLATION	To be alone, without social contact.
INTELLIGENCE	The ability to learn, reason.
JAIL	A temporary holding facility for people awaiting trail or transfer to prison.

MEDIA	A means to communicate to the public through newspapers, television, radio, etc.
MODUS OPERANDI	A way of working or operating, especially related with crime.
MOOD	The personal emotional state.
NARCISSISM	Excessiveness of loving oneself.
NARCOTIC	Any extreme substance that cause a drug like feeling.
NEUROSIS	A psychological disorder that dominates the personality.
OBEDIENCE	Complying with authority.
OBSESSION	A taking over in the mind of an idea or feeling.
PARANOIA	Extreme distrust.
PATTERN	A continuous behavior.
PERSONALITY	A likable quality in a person.
PREJUDICE	An opinion formed without knowledge or proof.
PRIDE	Good self esteem and self respect.
PRISON	An institution built for holding convicted prisoners.

PSYCHE	The complete mental structure.
PSYCHOLOGIST	A person that studies psychology.
PSYCHOLOGY	The study of the mind and mental states.
RECIDIVISM	Continuous relapses, as in crime.
REHABILITATION	The practice of returning to normal condition.
SOCIETY	Grouped people associated together by shared interests.
STEREOTYPE	An idea that lacks originality.
STIMULANT	An illegal substance.
SUBCULTURE	A culture within a culture that could be similar.
TRAITS	A very distinguishable quality or characteristic.
TRANSFERENCE	To move a persons idea, a thing, or the person to another location.
VIOLENCE	Intense force that can cause personal injury.

Printed in the United States
73679LV00002B/23